The informed choice for the discerning wine lover

TOP 100 SOUTH AFRICAN
WINES & WINE LISTS
2012/13

Top 100 South African Wines 2012/13 (2nd ed.) © Top 100 SA Wines cc
All rights reserved.

Second edition published in 2012 by Top 100 SA Wines cc
Reg. No. 2011/011771/23

Text © Top 100 SA Wines cc, all rights reserved.
Published format © Top 100 SA Wines cc, all rights reserved.
Foreword © Robin von Holdt
Chairman's Review © Tim Atkin MW

PUBLISHER Top 100 SA wines cc
EDITOR Lorissa Bouwer
DESIGN & LAYOUT The Graphic Ballroom
CARTOGRAPHY © John Hall
REPRODUCTION The Graphic Ballroom

Printed and bound in South Africa by CTP

ISBN: 978 0 620 52990 7

2012 CHALLENGE CHAIRMAN Tim Atkin MW
2012 CHALLENGE JUDGES
Dr Jamie Goode, Richard Kershaw MW
Duncan Savage, Madeleine Stenwreth MW
Greg Sherwood MW, Monty Waldin

FUNCTIONS MANAGER Joanne McGilvray
TASTING DIRECTOR Higgo Jacobs
DATA MANAGER Cheryl Guile
LOGISTICS Ren Bootha

www.top100sawines.com

CONTENTS

It gives me tremendous pleasure to be able to share my thoughts on the second vintage of fine wine book **Top 100 SA Wines 2012/13.**

"De-myth the bunk" is our strapline that guides all activity at **Top 100 SA Wines**. The confetti of awards handed out in wine competitions are as valueless to consumers as junk mail is to you or me. Does anyone actually care about whether or not a wine was labelled a silver or bronze medal winner, or given two or three stars? I doubt that very much. Jargon and small print do not help consumers either. Thus was born the concept of **Top 100 SA Wines**. Focussed, simple and clear.

A year down the road, a number of milestones has already been achieved. The book is sold in the USA and Europe and is available throughout South Africa. **Top 100** winning wines have been showcased multiple times during 2011/12 both in South Africa and abroad.

Most importantly, the winning wines are largely sold out! This is great news for winning vineyards. That means that you, the wine lover, are now identifying and buying the finest wines in South Africa. That is the intention of this book. Your pleasure is to 'work' through 100 fine South African wines, pre-selected by a panel of the world's greatest tasters. Core to successfully identifying these great wines is professional judging. The MW-led international team applied the best protocols to aid selection and a seven-person panel worked for five days and nights to find you a new list of winning wines.

New developments in this edition include listing winning restaurants of the **Top 100 SA Wine List Challenge**, **QR codes** for each listed restaurant and wine making it easier to book or buy using your smartphone and **Best Value Awards** for winners who meet certain price points – good news for you in today's tough economic times.

We hope that you find the 2012/13 edition even more useful and that you enjoy hugely the new great wines and restaurant dining opportunities now presented for your benefit. Please share the great news with friends and family. We wish you pleasurable reading, tasting, drinking and dining.

Robin von Holdt
Top 100 SA Wines

Welcome to the second edition of **Top 100 SA Wines**.

Top 100 SA Wines is based on South Africa's finest wines. This book features only the 100 winning wines from all the wines that entered into the prestigious annual **Top 100 Wine Challenge 2012/13**. The sole aim of the Challenge and this book is to assist you, the wine lover, to find great wines easily that you can enjoy now, or cellar with total confidence for later consumption. South Africa's finest wines are now positioned for your benefit with clarity, vigour and integrity.

The international market for fine wine is challenging and sometimes difficult to navigate. South African fine wines are on the up, both with regards to quality as well as quantity. Discerning consumers who use this book are now equipped to easily identify, find and purchase the best wine with absolute confidence. This edition also includes consistency recognition for vineyards that accumulate the most number of winning wines over all Challenge years.

In this edition we also introduce readers to a number of fine awarded restaurants whose wine lists were entered and judged by an expert panel of sommeliers arranged by **Top 100**. Four levels of awards were granted as well as a Best Value Award. Contact details and listing by region aids when planning journeys or holidays.

The 100 wines identified on the following pages represent the pinnacle of South African fine wines today. Consumers may now confidently purchase any of these awarded wines. They can be enjoyed today or cellared with certainty.

In addition to producing the definitive annual book of the **Top 100 SA Wines**, readers also now have access to:

· www.top100sawines.com, a current wine-centric website;
· visit the website diary for details on events throughout the year;
· info@top100sawines.com for wine advice or queries;
· Top 100 SA Wines private tasting events;
· Top 100 SA Wine tours for expert-led, inside-track bespoke tours;
· Top 100 SA Wines gifts and gift vouchers.

We are keen to receive your feedback and suggestions to help further enhance the book and its content for the benefit of readers. Please share your thoughts with the team on **www.top100sawines.com**

Whatever your level of interest in or love of fine wine may be, you can now identify and purchase any of the winning **Top 100 SA wines**. The book offers current information on the alphabetically listed winning wines, together with additional wine related and industry information.

Each wine is afforded two full pages which include QR codes, contact details, tasting hours and GPS co-ordinates. Wine details include vinification and maturation, oaking regime and ageing potential together with the winemaker's notes. Wine label images assist easy identification. Incisive comments from the Challenge judges summarise their views. Personalise your book with your own notes in the space provided.

Wine Challenge statistics and data are shared, enabling you to easily find your favourite wine. You can also find each winning vineyard identified with differentiated yellow dots set in the full colour maps.

The restaurant section is equally user-friendly. It lists all winners whose wine lists won an award in the **Wine List Challenge**. Restaurants are listed by award level as well as by location to enable easy use.

Grape cultivar abbreviations used in this guide:

Barbera	Barb	Pinotage	Ptage
Cabernet Franc	Cab Fr	Riesling	Ries
Cabernet Sauvignon	Cab Sauv	Paarl Riesling	P Ries
Carignan	Carig	Roobernet	Roob
Chardonnay	Chard	Roussanne	Rouss
Chenin Blanc	Chen Bl	Ruby Cabernet	Ruby C
Cinsaut	Cins	Sangiovese	Sang
Colombard	Cbard	Sauvignon Blanc	Sauv B
Cornifesto	Cfesto	Semillon	Sem
Gamay	Gamay	Shiraz	Shiraz
Gewürztraminer	Gewürz	Souzão	Souzão
Grenache	Gren	Sylvaner	Sylv
Hanepoot	Hanep	Tannat	Tann
Malbec	Malb	Tempranillo	Temp
Merlot	Merl	Tinta Amarela	Tinta A
Mourvedre	Mourv	Tinta Barocca	Tinta B
Muscadel	Musc	Tinta Francisca	Tinta F
Nebbiolo	Nebb	Tinta Roriz	Tinta R
Nouvelle	Nouv	Touriga Nacional	Tour N
Petit Verdot	Pet V	Verdelho	Verd
Pinot Grigio	Pin G	Viognier	Viog
Pinot Noir	Pinot	Zinfandel	Zin

calm in **chaos**

When in Cape Town
Refining the art of leisure
Calming life's tempo
Striking the right chords
Fine Jazz Fine Classics Fine Radio

FINE MUSIC RADIO
101.3

The **Top 100 SA Wine Challenge** is a world-class judged event held in Cape Town, South Africa. This is the definitive moment in South Africa's fine wine calendar; it is also the first annual calendar event. The Challenge provides talented South African winemakers with the opportunity to enter their fine wines. The objective is simple – identify South Africa's best wines and then share these facts with the public. The Challenge is open to all producers and free market principles apply. It is up to each producer to enact their entries.

Top 100 SA Wine Challenge provides an independent, objective and professional rating of all the entered wines. The two judging panels are made up of the highest quality international and South African experts. The MW-led panel of judges selects only the **Top 100 SA Wines** by final score from all judged entries. These winning 100 wines are showcased in this book.

Wines are tasted in categories, thus like is compared with like. Regardless of cultivar or category, only the top-scoring 100 wines come through at the end of the five-day judgement week. These wines are rightfully capped as South Africa's **Top 100** wines. Winning wines are then listed alphabetically in this book. Given the rigour of the tasting and assessing, wine scores or rankings are deemed unnecessary and are not provided. This is the definitive 'club' of finest South African wines in 2012/13.

Lynne Sherriff MW, South African Master of Wine and currently Chairman of the Institute of Masters of Wine, said of **Top 100 SA Wines:** *"The decision to draw upon the experience and knowledge of internationally renowned Masters of Wine as judges is a clear commitment to quality and will ensure that the process is rigorous."*

Eric Asimov, *NY Times*: *"Getting the word out about high-quality SA wine."*

Tim Atkin MW, author and judge: *"Top 100 SA Wines is one of the most exciting projects I have ever been involved with."*

Sam Harrop MW, author and consultant: *"It's a world-class event. Top 100 SA Wines have thought of everything. Expect great results."*

Top 100 SA Wine Challenge has developed a unique protocol that is recognised to be of the highest order. This is distinct and sets it apart and above any other similar event. It is at the pinnacle of leading global 'best practice.'

Top 100 SA Wine Challenge protocols include the following:

- All wines are tasted unsighted, a minimum of twice.
- Red wines, fortified and ports are served at approximately 19°C.
- White, rosé and dessert wines are served at approximately 13°C.
- Sparkling wines are served at approximately 7°C.
- All wines are tasted both decanted (12 hours red / 2 hours white) as well as from the bottle (15 minutes). Judges are aware of these duplicate wines to assist them in their accurate assessment.
- Separation – no dialogue is allowed during tasting sessions.
- High-scoring wines can be tasted up to a total of three times.

Transparency and credibility are both key values that underpin the reputation of the Top 100 SA Wine Challenge. Thus, the full tasting methodology is published and available on www.top100sawines.com

Top 100 SA Wines retains the service of a dedicated professional Tasting Director for each Wine Challenge event. Higgo Jacobs again fulfilled this role in 2012. Higgo was assisted by a team who provided logistical support. The event is pre-planned with great detail and accuracy. This forethought enables the wines to show at their best and also allows protection of palate fatigue for judges.

Ultimately, it is the respect that is demonstrated to all stakeholders and to the wines themselves that ensures that all entered wines have an equal and best chance to gain entry onto the winner's podium.

Good Corporate Governance

Careful international study and evaluation of wine competition and general governance has influenced the direction and practices adopted by **Top 100 SA Wines**. The intention is to showcase best practice where often vested interests can blur the boundaries of independence and integrity. Transparency of protocol, methodology and results are core to this approach.

Governance of the **Top 100 SA Wine Challenge** is compelling in that commercial interests are distinct and separate from the judging process and from the judges themselves. No employee of the company is eligible for any judging role and vice versa. Judges have a clear mandate and have a professional responsibility to discharge for which they are paid a professional fee.

Auditor Statement: Top 100 SA Wine Challenge 2012/13

Confirmatory statement of audit:

We take pleasure in confirming that the results of the Top 100 SA Wine Challenge 2012/13 are to our satisfaction.

The audit report is available for inspection at:
www.top100sawines.com/audit
or may be requested directly from the auditors.

GEORGE WILLIS + Co

G Willis and Co C.A. (SA)
PO Box 31145, Tokai, 7966
Tel: 021 712 0451
Fax: 021 712 4528

Getting a new competition off the ground is a considerable achievement, requiring courage, tenacity and no little investment. That's why I was delighted to be associated with the inaugural Top 100 SA Wine Challenge last year and why I have come back to lend my support to what is fast becoming an established feature of the Cape wine scene.

I am fortunate enough to judge wines professionally all over the world and the Top 100 Challenge is one of the best-organised tastings I know. The ambience, the staff, the glasses, the temperature of the wines, the size of the flights and the chance to compare decanted "reference" samples all make this a first-class event.

Top 100 is judged with integrity. Any competition relies first and foremost on the talent and experience of its judges and, as chairman, I was able to draw on the considerable abilities of a group of brilliant panellists. It goes without saying that there are no conflicts of interest. The one winemaker on our team was not allowed to judge the wine that his winery entered.

Blind tasting is fundamental to the integrity of Top 100, as is the reinforced Chinese wall between the administration and the tasters. None of us on the tasting floor knows the identity of wineries that have entered the competition, let alone the identities of individual wines. I am delighted that the event has been audited this year, making it even more professional.

The other thing that makes this competition different is that we take our time and discuss each wine in depth. No panel tastes more than 70 wines in a day. My job is to make sure that the panels are working to the same standard, but other than that it is the judges who make the decisions.

I am a huge fan, both of South Africa and its best wines, having visited the country more than a dozen times and marrying a Capetonian. I am proud of the Top 100 and what it has achieved in two years. Here's to the future. And to the enjoyment of some great Top 100 wines.

Tim Atkin MW

Top 100 SA Wines again sourced only the highest level of judges for the 2012/13 Challenge. International experts were present from South Africa's key export markets. They were selected for their respected reputations and sharp, educated palates bringing accuracy and objectivity once again to this prestigious event.

Winning wines now have global prestige and relevance as a result of their awarded performance. Typical qualities of winning wines include poise, elegance, fruit clarity, complexity and balance. These are the characters of fine wines.

Tim Atkin MW acted as Chair for the second year running bringing rigour and consistency to the Challenge. Two Deputies chaired their respective judging panels. The two panels each comprised a South African and an international judge, with one of them being MW qualified.

2012 JUDGING PANEL OVERVIEW

CHAIR	
Tim Atkin MW	
PANEL A	**PANEL B**
DEPUTY CHAIR	*DEPUTY CHAIR*
Jamie Goode	Richard Kershaw MW
&	&
Greg Sherwood MW	Madeleine Stenwreth MW
Duncan Savage	Monty Waldin

Tim Atkin MW (UK)
Chair

Tim is a UK-based wine journalist with an international following. He is the Wine Editor at Large of *Off Licence News*, wine columnist for *Woman and Home*, writes for *The World of Fine Wine* and *The Economist's Intelligent Life* and appears regularly as a BBC wine expert.
www.timatkin.com

"Top 100 showcases many of South Africa's best wines."

Jamie Goode (UK)
Deputy Chair

London-based wine writer, currently wine columnist for *The Sunday Express*. He won the 2007 Glenfiddich Wine Writer of the Year award and contributes regularly to *World of Fine Wine*, *Wines and Vines*, *Wine Business International*, *Sommelier Journal* and *Decanter*.
www.wineanorak.com

"Rigorous & in-depth. Quality of entries is reassuringly high."

Greg Sherwood MW (UK)

As Marketing Manager for fine wines from 2000-2006 and now Senior Wine Buyer for fine wines at Handford Wines in South Kensington, London, Greg has had the opportunity to buy, sell and taste some of the most finely crafted and sought after wines in the world on a daily basis.
www.mastersofwine.org

"The cream always rises to the top!"

Duncan Savage (SA)

Constantly experimenting, Duncan is whole-heartedly striving to attain his goal of establishing Cape Point Vineyards as one of the world's leading Sauvignon Blanc producers. This is Duncan's second year judging for Top 100.

www.capepointvineyards.co.za

"Fantastic wines entered; a defining result."

Richard Kershaw MW (SA)
Deputy Chair

Recently awarded the title Master of Wine (MW), Richard is now embarking on his own venture, Richard Kershaw Wines, having been the previous cellarmaster of Mulderbosch. UK-born, Richard studied in London and worked as a chef before moving into the wine trade.
www.rikipedia.co

"Crucial benchmarking competition to delineate top Cape wine."

Madeleine Stenwreth MW (Sweden)

Global consultant for high-profile wine producers and importers, Madeleine has judged at Decanter WWA, Argentina Wine Awards and Royal Adelaide Wine Show. Her work experience includes wine buyer, restaurant management and sommelier.

www.madeleinestenwreth.se

"Cutting-edge ... First and foremost rewards the consumer."

Monty Waldin (Italy)

Monty became the first wine writer and broadcaster to specialise in organic/ biodynamic wine. In addition to biodynamic consulting worldwide, his client Burklin Wolf is Germany's largest. Monty has judged at the IWC and Decanter.

"Thoughtfully organised tasting of South Africa's best wines."

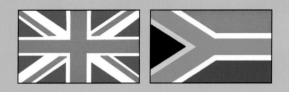

Total Entries	2012	2011
Vineyards entered	136	135
Average number of wines entered per vineyard	2.84	3
Total entries	386	411
Declined	13	15
	Unpaid	Not bottled in time
	Wines not delivered	Wine not available
	Forms not completed	Operational reasons
	No WSR4A number	
Withdrawn	7	6
	Not bottled in time	Not bottled in time
	Stock levels	Wine not available
		Operational reasons
Wines tasted	366	390

Entries	2012	2011
Red	221	234
White	129	151
MCC	23	15
Natural sweet	4	6
Port	9	5
TOTAL	386	411

Top 100 Winners	2012	2011
Red	51	43
White	38	46
MCC	4	5
Natural sweet	3	2
Port	4	4
TOTAL	100	100

Entries by Wine of Origin classification 2012	
Banghoek	10
Bot River	5
Calitzdorp	4
Cape Agulhas	8
Cape Point	1
Cederberg	15
Central Orange, Northern Cape	1
Citrusdal Mountains	1
Coastal	21
Constantia	15
Darling	6
Durbanville	11
Elgin	13
Elim	3
Franschhoek	15
Goudini	3
Hemel-en-Aarde Valley	3
Jonkershoek Valley	1
Klein River	4
Outeniqua	1
Overberg	1
Paarl	15
Piekenierskloof	3
Robertson	15
Simonsberg, Paarl	6
Simonsberg, Stellenbosch	4
Stellenbosch	103
Sutherland, Karoo	1
Swartberg	14
Tulbagh	5
Upper Hemel-en-Aarde Valley	6
Upper-Langkloof	4
Voor Paardeberg	10
Walker Bay	5
Wellington	9
Western Cape	38
Worcester	6
TOTAL	**386**

Reasons producers declined to enter from most to least:

- Tight economic times mandated budget cuts
- Bottle shock/wine not ready
- Only enter international competitions
- Did not win an award last year so am not entering this year
- Harvest time – too busy
- Left it too late and missed deadline

Challenge logistics:

- On average 120 wines tasted per day
- Each panel tasted approximately 60 wines, twice, per day
- Each wine enjoyed approximately 6 minutes of each judge's attention. Together with Chair's time approximately 20 minutes in total
- Total faults
  - Cork taint – 18
  - Oxidised – 1
  - Brett – 3
  - Reductive – 3
  - Mercaptan – 1
  - Volatile acidity – 1
  - 14 non-fault repours
  - 900 Riedel glasses on site
  - 240 decanters on site
  - 600 glasses washed daily – 6-person hand wash team
  - 4 dedicated pourers
  - 2 panel assistants / observers on site
  - 1 Chartered Accountant auditor

The following wines have collectively become the Top 100 SA Wines 2012/13. The winning wines are showcased alphabetically over the following pages. Here we have categorised the winners firstly by white/red/others and then by cultivar/blend.

Other red cultivars

Red wine blends
Bordeaux red blend

Rhône-style blend

Other red blend

Others
Méthode Cap Classique

Natural sweet wines

Port

Winning white wines ≤ R100

Chardonnay
Alvi's Drift AD Chardonnay 2011	R 99
Glenwood Chardonnay Vigneron's Selection 2010	R 95
Longridge Chardonnay 2009	R 89

Chenin Blanc
Jean Daneel Chenin Blanc 2010	R 96
Jordan Chenin Blanc 2011	R 97
Kanu KCB Chenin Blanc 2009	R 85
Mulderbosch Chenin Blanc Steen op Hout 2010	R 59

Other white cultivars
Alvi's Drift Viognier 2011	R 40
Jordan The Real McCoy Riesling 2010	R 100

White blends
Allée Bleue Isabeau 2011	R 70
Alvi's Drift AD CVC 2011	R 99

Winning red wines ≤ R120

Cabernet Sauvignon
Eikendal Cabernet Sauvignon 2009	R 85

Pinotage
Allée Bleue Pinotage 2009	R 106
Swartland Winery Bush Vine Pinotage 2010	R 98

Shiraz
Christina van Loveren Shiraz 2010	R 105
Elgin Heights Shiraz 2010	R 90
Elgin Vintners Shiraz 2008	R 99
Saronsberg Provenance Shiraz 2010	R 110
Swartland Winery Bush Vine Shiraz 2010	R 98
Vondeling Baldrick Shiraz 2011	R 50

Other red cultivars
Calitzdorp Cellar Touriga Nacional 2010	R 32
Doolhof Wine Estate Signature Malbec 2010	R 115
Longridge Merlot 2008	R 107

Red blends
Ernie Els Big Easy 2010	R 120
Rickety Bridge The Foundation Stone 2010	R 85
Saronsberg Provenance Rooi 2010	R 110

Winning Méthode Cap Classique ≤ R100
Simonsig Kaapse Vonkel 2007	R 97

Winning Port wines ≤ R120
Bredell's Cape Vintage 2003	R 65
Calitzdorp Cellar Cape Ruby 2010	R 38

Prices quoted are approx retail price

CONSISTENCY RECOGNITION

In order to give the reader an idea of how consistent a vineyard has performed in accumulated Top 100 Challenges thus far (two years) we simply indicate the total number of winning wines that they have accumulated to date.

Name of Vineyard	Total	Name of Vineyard	Total
Cederberg Private Cellar	9	Anwilka Vineyard	2
Saronsberg Cellar	9	Bon Courage Wine Estate	2
Jordan Wine Estate	7	Boplaas Family Vineyards	2
Oldenburg Vineyards	5	Calitzdorp Cellar	2
Simonsig Estate	5	Creation Wines	2
Bosman Family Vineyards	4	De Krans	2
Klein Constantia	4	Flagstone	2
Lomond	4	Glenelly Cellars	2
Longridge	4	Ken Forrester Wines	2
Paul Cluver Wines	4	L'Avenir	2
Teddy Hall Wines	4	Le Riche	2
Tokara	4	MAN Vintners	2
Allée Bleue Wines	3	Miles Mossop Wines	2
Alvi's Drift Wines	3	Mvemve Raats	2
Boschendal Wines	3	Neethlingshof	2
Cape Point Vineyards	3	Overgaauw Wine Estate	2
Diemersdal Wine Estate	3	Quoin Rock Winery	2
Ernie Els Wines	3	Rickety Bridge Winery	2
Graham Beck Wines	3	Saxenburg Wine Estate	2
Groot Constantia	3	Stark-Condé	2
Hamilton Russell Vineyards	3	Steenberg	2
La Motte	3	Sumaridge Estate Wines	2
Mulderbosch	3	Swartland Winery	2
Rijk's Private Cellar	3	Zorgvliet Wines	2
Rustenberg Wines	3		
The Bernard Series	3		
Vondeling	3		

Bottled Inspiration

Producer Details

Vineyard/Producer	Allée Bleue Wines
Physical address	Intersection R45 & R310, Groot Drakenstein
Map page	271
GPS co-ordinates	S 33° 51′ 29.0″ E 018° 59′ 12.9″
Established	1690
Owner	Mr & Mrs Dauphin
Cellarmaster	n/a
Winemaker	Van Zyl du Toit
Viticulturist	Douw Willemse
First bottled vintage	2001
Area under vines	135 ha
Main varieties	Cab Sauv, Merl, Ptage, Shiraz, Chen Bl, Sauv B
Red : white ratio	60 : 40
Total bottle production	216 000

Contact Details

Tel	021 874 1021
Email	sonja.bester@alleebleue.com
Web	www.alleebleue.com
Tasting days & hours	Mon-Fri 9-5; Sat 10-5; Sun 10-4
Tasting fee	R 20 for 4 wines
Other attractions	Bistro, wedding & conference venues, accom

Personal Tasting Notes

Judges' Comments

Attractive and modern style with ripe tropical fruit, oriental spice, bold flavours and prominent oak which will, given time, integrate with fruit. Long finish.

Wine Details

Wine of origin	Western Cape		
Alcohol level	13.5%		
Residual Sugar g/L	2		
Total Acid g/L	5.8		
pH	3.42		
Closure type	Cork		
Single vineyard	n/a		
Grape varietals	Chard	Sem	Viog
Percentage	60%	36%	4%
Irrigated	yes	yes	yes
Farm method	n/a	n/a	n/a
Debut vintage	2001		
Total bottles produced	14 100		
Approx retail price	R 70		

Vinification	Grapes sourced from selected areas for their individuality. Harvested at night and stored in a cool room. Sorted, crushed and pressed the following day.
Oaking	French oak for 9 months.
Maturation	Natural ferment done on 50%, MLF done in barrel. Regular battonage. Aged on lees 9 months before blending and bottling.
Ageing potential	2-4 years

Winemaker Notes

Our flagship white wine. Pale straw hue with shades of green. Abundant citrus and dried apricot welcome you on the nose. Palate is silky with elegant flavours of summer fruits.

Producer Details

Vineyard/Producer	Allée Bleue Wines
Physical address	Intersection R45 & R310, Groot Drakenstein
Map page	271
GPS co-ordinates	S 33° 51′ 29.0″ E 018° 59′ 12.9″
Established	1690
Owner	Mr & Mrs Dauphin
Cellarmaster	n/a
Winemaker	Van Zyl du Toit
Viticulturist	Douw Willemse
First bottled vintage	2001
Area under vines	135 ha
Main varieties	Cab Sauv, Merl, Ptage, Shiraz, Chen Bl, Sauv B
Red : white ratio	60 : 40
Total bottle production	216 000

Contact Details

Tel	021 874 1021
Email	sonja.bester@alleebleue.com
Web	www.alleebleue.com
Tasting days & hours	Mon-Fri 9-5; Sat 10-5; Sun 10-4
Tasting fee	R 20 for 4 wines
Other attractions	Bistro, wedding & conference venues, accom

Personal Tasting Notes

Judges' Comments

A sexy, inviting, fresh aromatic nose leaping to notably forthright blackberry and apple crumble. Generously proportioned.

Wine Details

Wine of origin	Piekenierskloof
Alcohol level	15%
Residual Sugar g/L	2
Total Acid g/L	4.9
pH	3.9
Closure type	Cork
Single vineyard	n/a
Grape varietals	Ptage
Percentage	100%
Irrigated	yes
Farm method	n/a
Debut vintage	2000
Total bottles produced	11 886
Approx retail price	R 106

Vinification	Grapes sourced from selected mountain vineyards in the Piekenierskloof. Harvested, sorted, cooled and crushed. Then cold soaked for 4 days. Yeast inoculation.
Oaking	French oak for 14 months.
Maturation	French oak barrels: 60% new, 2nd and 3rd fill. 10% American oak also used.
Ageing potential	3-5 years

Winemaker Notes

Intense brick colour. Upfront fruit reminds of ripe cherries and strawberries followed by sweet vanilla pods and some liquorice. Palate is rich, soft and very elegant.

Producer Details

Vineyard/Producer	Alvi's Drift Wines International
Physical address	Scharpenhueval Road, Worcester
Map page	279
GPS co-ordinates	S 33° 46' 24.56" E 019° 31' 56.82"
Established	1928
Owner	Alvi and Johan van der Merwe & Linley Schultz
Cellarmaster	Henk Swart
Winemaker	Alvi van der Merwe
Viticulturist	Jan du Toit
First bottled vintage	2001
Area under vines	400 ha
Main varieties	Chen Bl, Sauv B, Chard, Cab Sauv, Merl, Shiraz
Red : white ratio	20 : 80
Total bottle production	100 000

Contact Details

Tel	023 340 4117
Email	linley@alvisdrift.co.za
Web	www.alvisdrift.co.za
Tasting days & hours	By appointment
Tasting fee	Complimentary
Other attractions	River, game, tours by appointment

Personal Tasting Notes

Judges' Comments

Ripe, rich pear and peach fruit with notes of melon and quince – fruit-forward with some spicy oak. Well balanced.

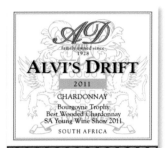

Wine Details

Wine of origin	Worcester
Alcohol level	13.4%
Residual Sugar g/L	4.5
Total Acid g/L	6.3
pH	3.2
Closure type	Synthetic
Single vineyard	n/a
Grape varietals	Chard
Percentage	100%
Irrigated	yes
Farm method	n/a
Debut vintage	2010
Total bottles produced	6 000
Approx retail price	R 99
Vinification	Grapes hand picked, crushed, cold settled, clean juice with cool fermentation.
Oaking	10 months in mixture of French and American barriques and hogsheads.
Maturation	Stored on lees in French and American hogsheads and barriques for 10 months. Battonage to add texture to the wine.
Ageing potential	5 years

Winemaker Notes

The wine has a nice straw colour with subtle and integrated oak on the nose. The palate is elegant yet full flavoured. Roasted nuts and peach fruit characters linger on the aftertaste.

Producer Details

Vineyard/Producer	Alvi's Drift Wines International
Physical address	Scharpenhueval Road, Worcester
Map page	279
GPS co-ordinates	S 33° 46' 24.56" E 019° 31' 56.82"
Established	1928
Owner	Alvi and Johan van der Merwe & Linley Schultz
Cellarmaster	Henk Swart
Winemaker	Alvi van der Merwe
Viticulturist	Jan du Toit
First bottled vintage	2001
Area under vines	400 ha
Main varieties	Chen Bl, Sauv B, Chard, Cab Sauv, Merl, Shiraz
Red : white ratio	20 : 80
Total bottle production	100 000

Contact Details

Tel	023 340 4117
Email	linley@alvisdrift.co.za
Web	www.alvisdrift.co.za
Tasting days & hours	By appointment
Tasting fee	Complimentary
Other attractions	River, game, tours by appointment

Personal Tasting Notes

Judges' Comments

Baked apple, honeyed botrytised influence, good quality caramel oak giving complex, nutty, waxy notes. Ripe, sweetness of fruit on the long aftertaste.

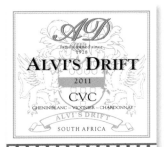

Wine Details

Wine of origin	Worcester		
Alcohol level	13.5%		
Residual Sugar g/L	4		
Total Acid g/L	6.4		
pH	3.2		
Closure type	Synthetic		
Single vineyard	n/a		
Grape varietals	Chen Bl	Viog	Chard
Percentage	60%	25%	15%
Irrigated	yes	yes	yes
Farm method	n/a	n/a	n/a
Debut vintage	2008		
Total bottles produced	8 000		
Approx retail price	R 99		

Vinification	Crushed, cold settled, clean juice, fermented in barrels.
Oaking	Oaked for 10 months in mixed barrels.
Maturation	Varietals aged separately on lees in barrels with battonage for 6 months.
Ageing potential	5 years

Winemaker Notes

A lovely, full-bodied and elegant blend with Chenin Blanc providing the base, Viogner the peach and apricot aromas and Chardonnay a nutty and balanced finish.

Producer Details

Vineyard/Producer	Alvi's Drift Wines International
Physical address	Scharpenhueval Road, Worcester
Map page	279
GPS co-ordinates	S 33° 46' 24.56" E 019° 31' 56.82"
Established	1928
Owner	Alvi and Johan van der Merwe & Linley Schultz
Cellarmaster	Henk Swart
Winemaker	Alvi van der Merwe
Viticulturist	Jan du Toit
First bottled vintage	2001
Area under vines	400 ha
Main varieties	Chen Bl, Sauv B, Chard, Cab Sauv, Merl, Shiraz
Red : white ratio	20 : 80
Total bottle production	100 000

Contact Details

Tel	023 340 4117
Email	linley@alvisdrift.co.za
Web	www.alvisdrift.co.za
Tasting days & hours	By appointment
Tasting fee	Complimentary
Other attractions	River, game, tours by appointment

Personal Tasting Notes

Judges' Comments

Intense dried pears, apricots, nectarine, pineapple blossom. Rich and creamy palate. Well made. Satisfying and dense. Pleasing.

Wine Details

Wine of origin	Worcester
Alcohol level	14%
Residual Sugar g/L	4
Total Acid g/L	6.5
pH	3.2
Closure type	Synthetic
Single vineyard	n/a
Grape varietals	Viog
Percentage	100%
Irrigated	yes
Farm method	n/a
Debut vintage	2010
Total bottles produced	10 000
Approx retail price	R 40
Vinification	Crushed, cold settled, clean juice, cold fermented.
Oaking	Oaked for 10 months in mixed barrels.
Maturation	Matured on lees for 8 months.
Ageing potential	5 years

Winemaker Notes

The wine is unusually restrained for a Viognier, lovely elegant apricot and peach fruit characters are complemented by a lingering finish.

Producer Details

Vineyard/Producer	Anwilka Vineyard
Physical address	Raithby-Annandale Road, Somerset West
Map page	274-275
GPS co-ordinates	S 34° 1' 8.77" E 018° 48' 9.54"
Established	2005
Owner	LD Jooste, B Prats & H de Boüard
Cellarmaster	B Prats & H de Boüard
Winemaker	Jean du Plessis
Viticulturist	Johan Wiese
First bottled vintage	2005
Area under vines	40 ha
Main varieties	Shiraz, Cab Sauv, Merl, Pet V
Red : white ratio	100% red
Total bottle production	150 000

Contact Details

Tel	021 842 3225
Email	jean@anwilka.com
Web	www.anwilka.com
Tasting days & hours	By appointment
Tasting fee	Complimentary
Other attractions	n/a

Personal Tasting Notes

Judges' Comments

Thick inky colour, some generous flavours – liquorice, plum, dark cherry, white pepper, dark berries. Very well matched by some top-quality oak. Weighty and serious.

ANWILKA

STELLENBOSCH

SOUTH AFRICA

2009

Wine Details

Wine of origin	Stellenbosch	
Alcohol level	14.5%	
Residual Sugar g/L	2.1	
Total Acid g/L	5.3	
pH	3.6	
Closure type	Cork	
Single vineyard	n/a	
Grape varietals	Shiraz	Cab Sauv
Percentage	56%	44%
Irrigated	yes	yes
Farm method	n/a	n/a
Debut vintage	2005	
Total bottles produced	4 300	
Approx retail price	R 370	

Vinification	Bunch sorting in vineyard, berry sorting in cellar. AF in stainless steel tronconic tanks, post maceration on skins, basket pressed, then to French oak barrel.
Oaking	French oak for 13 months.
Maturation	MLF in combination of tank and wood. Batches matured separately, blending and fining just before bottling. Unfiltered.
Ageing potential	8 years

Winemaker Notes

Perhaps best Anwilka made. Nose: black cherry, blueberry, discreet eucalypt, well-integrated oak. Palate: supple, textured tannins, fine acidity. Chocolate finish with elegant toasted notes.

Producer Details

Vineyard/Producer	Avontuur Estate
Physical address	R44, Somerset West
Map page	274
GPS co-ordinates	S 34° 1' 33.2" E 018° 49' 23.8"
Established	1850
Owner	Taberer Family
Cellarmaster	n/a
Winemaker	Jan van Rooyen
Viticulturist	Pippa Mickleburgh
First bottled vintage	1990
Area under vines	80 ha
Main varieties	Cab Sauv, Merl, Ptage, Shiraz, Cab Fr, Pinot
Red : white ratio	60 : 40
Total bottle production	240 000

Contact Details

Tel	021 855 3450
Email	info@avontuurestate.co.za
Web	www.avontuurestate.co.za
Tasting days & hours	Mon-Fri 8.30-5;
	Sat & Sun 9-4
Tasting fee	R 20 for 5 wines
Other attractions	Restaurant

Personal Tasting Notes

Judges' Comments

Vivid and fresh with fresh rasberry and cherry fruit. Supple and juicy with appealing ripe fruit.

Wine Details

Wine of origin	Stellenbosch
Alcohol level	14%
Residual Sugar g/L	4.3
Total Acid g/L	6.2
pH	3.51
Closure type	Cork
Single vineyard	n/a
Grape varietals	Shiraz
Percentage	100%
Irrigated	no
Farm method	n/a
Debut vintage	2008
Total bottles produced	6 000
Approx retail price	R 130

Vinification	Harvested at full ripeness, destemmed, cold soaked and inoculated. Pumped over regularly.
Oaking	French and American oak for 15 months.
Maturation	In French and American oak barrels for 15 months. 1st and 2nd fill.
Ageing potential	5 years

Winemaker Notes

Ripe dark fruit aromas with spicy undertones of clove and coriander. Full-bodied mouthfeel with ripe flavours reminiscent of spicy dark fruit cake. Well-rounded, integrated wood nuances.

Producer Details

Vineyard/Producer	Bon Courage Wine Estate
Physical address	R317, Robertson
Map page	280
GPS co-ordinates	S 33° 50′ 43.8″ E 019° 57′ 38.0″
Established	1927
Owner	André Bruwer
Cellarmaster	Jacques Bruwer
Winemaker	Jacques Bruwer
Viticulturist	André Bruwer
First bottled vintage	1983
Area under vines	250 ha
Main varieties	Cab Sauv, Shiraz, Chard, Cbard
Red : white ratio	60 : 40
Total bottle production	Not specified

Contact Details

Tel	023 626 4178
Email	wine@boncourage.co.za
Web	www.boncourage.co.za
Tasting days & hours	Mon-Fri 8-5; Sat 9-3
Tasting fee	Complimentary; R 10 pp for groups of more than 10
Other attractions	Restaurant with a children's play area

Personal Tasting Notes

Judges' Comments

A commendably linear sparkling wine with complex nougat, brioche and rich creamy characters and very good autolytic finish.

CAP CLASSIQUE
JACQUES BRUÉRE
BRUT RESERVE 2007
FERMENTÉ EN BOUTEILLE

750ml   SPARKLING WINE   12.5%
    W.O. ROBERTSON
A177   WINE OF SOUTH AFRICA   Alc.Vol.

Wine Details

Wine of origin	Robertson	
Alcohol level	12.64%	
Residual Sugar g/L	6.3	
Total Acid g/L	8.2	
pH	3.33	
Closure type	Cork	
Single vineyard	Yes	
Grape varietals	Pinot	Chard
Percentage	60%	40%
Irrigated	yes	yes
Farm method	n/a	org
Debut vintage	1991	
Total bottles produced	2 050	
Approx retail price	R 110	

Vinification	On lees 8 months. Bottled, laid down 36-48 months. After 2nd fermentation, wine riddled by hand in riddling racks for 3 weeks. Disgorged. On the cork 9 months.
Oaking	10% of the wine is barrel fermented. French oak for 10 months.
Maturation	n/a
Ageing potential	5 years

Winemaker Notes

Aroma of peach with hints of citrus. Rich creamy flavours, a good combination of fruitiness and yeastiness. The palate has both intensity and delicacy. Crisp with a lingering finish.

Producer Details

Vineyard/Producer	Boplaas Family Vineyards
Physical address	2 Saayman Street, Calitzdorp
Map page	283
GPS co-ordinates	S 33° 32′ 8.0″ E 021° 41′ 1.9″
Established	1880
Owner	Carel Nel
Cellarmaster	Carel Nel
Winemaker	Margaux Nel
Viticulturist	Pieter Terblanch
First bottled vintage	1970
Area under vines	70 ha
Main varieties	Ptage, Shiraz, Merl, Cab Sauv, Tour N, Tinta B
Red : white ratio	40% red, 30% white, 20% port, 10% dessert wine
Total bottle production	Not specified

Contact Details

Tel	044 213 3326
Email	winemaker@boplaas.co.za
Web	www.boplaas.co.za
Tasting days & hours	Mon-Fri 8-5; Sat 9-3; Sun (selected) 11-2
Tasting fee	R 20 for 5 tastings
Other attractions	Vineyard walking trail, Ring of Rocks (stone circle)

Personal Tasting Notes

Judges' Comments

Sweet and open with raising fruit and some spiciness. Toffee and caramel notes. Very stylish.

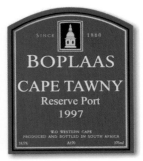

Wine Details

Wine of origin	Western Cape	
Alcohol level	18.6%	
Residual Sugar g/L	109	
Total Acid g/L	5.3	
pH	3.46	
Closure type	Cork, synthetic & cork T-top	
Single vineyard	n/a	
Grape varietals	Tinta B	Tour N
Percentage	85%	15%
Irrigated	no	no
Farm method	n/a	n/a
Debut vintage	2010	
Total bottles produced	1 200	
Approx retail price	R 150	

Vinification	Harvested at 26°B from Tinta B vines, yield 6 tons/ha. Must fermented in traditional open fermenters, punch downs every 4 hours. Fortified using Potstill brandy.
Oaking	Old pipes for 12 months.
Maturation	Aged for 12–18 months in very old barrels.
Ageing potential	Aged in the barrels; enjoy now

Winemaker Notes

Spice, treacle/caramel, bitter orange, wafts of spirit on the bouquet. Complex palate, roast nuts, hints of cinnamon and allspice. Lingering dry finish with treacle and spice undertones.

Producer Details

Vineyard/Producer	Boplaas Family Vineyards
Physical address	2 Saayman Street, Calitzdorp
Map page	283
GPS co-ordinates	S 33° 32' 8.0" E 021° 41' 1.9"
Established	1880
Owner	Carel Nel
Cellarmaster	Carel Nel
Winemaker	Margaux Nel
Viticulturist	Pieter Terblanch
First bottled vintage	1970
Area under vines	70 ha
Main varieties	Ptage, Shiraz, Merl, Cab Sauv, Tour N, Tinta B
Red : white ratio	40% red, 30% white, 20% port, 10% dessert
Total bottle production	Not specified

Contact Details

Tel	044 213 3326
Email	winemaker@boplaas.co.za
Web	www.boplaas.co.za
Tasting days & hours	Mon-Fri 8-5; Sat 9-3; Sun (selected) 11-2
Tasting fee	R 20 for 5 tastings
Other attractions	Vineyard walking trail, Ring of Rocks (stone circle)

Personal Tasting Notes

Judges' Comments

Pure sweet blackberry and black cherry fruit. Intense, direct and structured. Impressive with potential.

Wine Details

Wine of origin	Western Cape		
Alcohol level	18%		
Residual Sugar g/L	95		
Total Acid g/L	5.6		
pH	3.6		
Closure type	Cork		
Single vineyard	n/a		
Grape varietals	Tour N	Tinta B	Souzão
Percentage	85%	13%	2%
Irrigated	yes	yes	yes
Farm method	n/a	n/a	n/a
Debut vintage	2011		
Total bottles produced	3 000		
Approx retail price	R 200		

Vinification	Grapes harvested at 26ºB with a yield of 5 tons/ha. Young Touriga Nacional Vines planted in '97 and old Tinta Barocca Vines planted in '68.
Oaking	Lightly oaked in French oak for 18 months.
Maturation	Aged for 12–18 months in very old barrels.
Ageing potential	50 years

Winemaker Notes

Beautiful ripe rich tannins, lots of fruit and lingering aftertaste.

Producer Details

Vineyard/Producer	Bellingham Wines & Boschendal Wines
Physical address	Boschendal - R310, Pniel Road, Groot Drakenstein
Map page	271
GPS co-ordinates	Boschendal - S 33° 52′ 27.5″Ð E 018° 58′ 34.4″
Established	n/a
Owner	DGB (Pty) Ltd
Cellarmaster	n/a
Winemaker	JC Bekker (group winemaker)
Viticulturist	Stephan Joubert
First bottled vintage	n/a
Area under vines	n/a
Main varieties	n/a
Red : white ratio	n/a
Total bottle production	n/a

Contact Details

Tel	021 870 4200
Email	vanessas@dgb.co.za
Web	www.dgb.co.za
Tasting days & hours	Boschendal - Mon-Sun 8.30-4.30 (winter), 10-6 (summer)
Tasting fee	Boschendal - R 20 (5 wines), R 30 (conducted tasting)
Other attractions	n/a

Personal Tasting Notes

Judges' Comments

Authoratative wine with depth, ripeness and complexity. A good mix of fruit and floral notes with very pleasant autolytic character. Tightly structured and long finish.

Wine Details

Wine of origin	Coastal	
Alcohol level	12.5%	
Residual Sugar g/L	7.1	
Total Acid g/L	7.3	
pH	3.36	
Closure type	Cork & synthetic	
Single vineyard	n/a	
Grape varietals	Chard	Pinot
Percentage	54%	46%
Irrigated	yes	yes
Farm method	n/a	n/a
Debut vintage	2006	
Total bottles produced	60 000	
Approx retail price	R 125	

Vinification	Juice cold settled 48 hours, racked and fermented at 16°C. Left on primary lees until blending. 2nd fermentation in bottle with addition of liqueur de tirage.
Oaking	Unoaked.
Maturation	Extended maturation on the lees for 24 months.
Ageing potential	Not specified

Winemaker Notes

Fresh green fruit with hints of citrus supported by discreet almond biscotti and brioche. A full and creamy mounthfeel with elegant minerality, good balance and a seamless finish.

Producer Details

Vineyard/Producer	Bosman Family Vineyards
Physical address	Lelienfontein Farm, Hexberg Road, Bovlei, Wellington
Map page	272-273
GPS co-ordinates	S 33° 37' 36.3" E 019° 1' 52.1"
Established	2007
Owner	JC Bosman
Cellarmaster	Petrus Bosman
Winemaker	Corlea Fourie
Viticulturist	Heinie Nel
First bottled vintage	2004
Area under vines	250 ha
Main varieties	Chen Bl, Cab Sauv, Merl, Ptage
Red : white ratio	85 : 15
Total bottle production	102 000

Contact Details

Tel	021 873 3170
Email	cbotha@vinegrowers.co.za
Web	www.bosmanwines.com
Tasting days & hours	By appointment
Tasting fee	Complimentary
Other attractions	Vine nursery

Personal Tasting Notes

Judges' Comments

Floral violets, fleshy palate, fine grained in terms of fruit and oak tannin. A charming yet serious wine with plenty of potential.

BOSMAN

Family Vineyards

ERFENIS

2010

LELIENFONTEIN WELLINGTON SOUTH AFRICA

ANNO 1699

Wine Details

Wine of origin	Wellington				
Alcohol level	14.7%				
Residual Sugar g/L	2.5				
Total Acid g/L	5.5				
pH	3.62				
Closure type	Cork				
Single vineyard	n/a				
Grape varietals	Ptage	Pet V	Cab Fr	Shiraz	Cins
Percentage	30%	22.5%	22.5%	22.5%	2.5%
Irrigated	yes	yes	yes	yes	yes
Farm method	fair	fair	fair	fair	fair
Debut vintage	2010				
Total bottles produced	1 289				
Approx retail price	R 300				

Vinification	The components were chosen from the top barrels for the varieties from which it was made. It was blended to be representative of the finest of our 2010 crop.
Oaking	French barrels for 18 months.
Maturation	Matured in small French oak barrels for 18 months.
Ageing potential	2-7 years

Winemaker Notes

Dark, rich flavours of mulberry and cranberries with underlying spice. A special wine for special decanting and enjoyment.

Producer Details

Vineyard/Producer	Bosman Family Vineyards
Physical address	Lelienfontein Farm, Hexberg Road, Bovlei, Wellington
Map page	272-273
GPS co-ordinates	S 33° 37′ 36.3″ E 019° 1′ 52.1″
Established	2007
Owner	JC Bosman
Cellarmaster	Petrus Bosman
Winemaker	Corlea Fourie
Viticulturist	Heinie Nel
First bottled vintage	2004
Area under vines	250 ha
Main varieties	Chen Bl, Cab Sauv, Merl, Ptage
Red : white ratio	85 : 15
Total bottle production	102 000

Contact Details

Tel	021 873 317
Email	cbotha@vinegrowers.co.za
Web	www.bosmanwines.com
Tasting days & hours	By appointment
Tasting fee	Complimentary
Other attractions	Vine nursery

Personal Tasting Notes

Judges' Comments

Rich melon and buttered toast notes on the nose. The palate is fresh with richer melon notes as well as a hint of honey and cream.

Wine Details

Wine of origin	Wellington
Alcohol level	13.72%
Residual Sugar g/L	2.5
Total Acid g/L	6.7
pH	3.17
Closure type	Cork
Single vineyard	Yes, Gesamentlike Wei
Grape varietals	Chen Bl
Percentage	100%
Irrigated	no
Farm method	fair
Debut vintage	2010
Total bottles produced	2 300
Approx retail price	R 175

Vinification	Grapes harvested and whole bunch pressed. Part natural ferment. Kept on its lees for 9 months before bottling.
Oaking	French barrels for 9 months.
Maturation	Barrel fermented and matured in Latour French oak. Part natural fermentation. Maturation for 9 months, regular stirring.
Ageing potential	2-5 years

Winemaker Notes

Features in our Special Vineyard Selection – those wines which speak of a place where it is rooted.

Producer Details

Vineyard/Producer	JP Bredell Wines
Physical address	Faure Waterscheme Road, Firgrove
Map page	274-275
GPS co-ordinates	n/a
Established	1995
Owner	Anton Bredell
Cellarmaster	Anton Bredell
Winemaker	Jacques Bredell & Denzil Tromp
Viticulturist	Jacques Bredell
First bottled vintage	1991
Area under vines	10.5 ha
Main varieties	Ptage, Cab Sauv, Pinot, Merl
Red : white ratio	100% red
Total bottle production	10 000

Contact Details

Tel	021 842 2478
Email	info@bredellwine.co.za
Web	n/a
Tasting days & hours	Mon-Fri 9-5
Tasting fee	Complimentary
Other attractions	n/a

Personal Tasting Notes

Judges' Comments

Nicely elegant with sweet blackberry fruit. Smooth and pure but with some grippy tannins.

Wine Details

Wine of origin	Stellenbosch			
Alcohol level	20%			
Residual Sugar g/L	81.5			
Total Acid g/L	4.2			
pH	3.98			
Closure type	Cork			
Single vineyard	n/a			
Grape varietals	Tinta B	Tour N	Tour F	Souzão
Percentage	43%	9%	19.5%	28.5%
Irrigated	no	no	no	no
Farm method	n/a	n/a	n/a	n/a
Debut vintage	2005			
Total bottles produced	12 200			
Approx retail price	R 65			

Vinification	Each cultivar harvested, fermented, aged separately. Skins forming the cap manually punched through every 2 hours. Wine separated from skins, fortification.
Oaking	French oak barrels for 24 months.
Maturation	2 years individual ageing in old 500L oak barrels, cultivars blended.
Ageing potential	20-30 years

Winemaker Notes

Dark crimson, voluptuously rich. Christmas pudding, dried fruit, mocha, mint and spice. Stilton cheese and roasted nuts to enhance the balance, the dry finish and the lingering aftertaste.

Producer Details

Vineyard/Producer	Calitzdorp Cellar
Physical address	Andries Pretorius Street, Calitzdorp
Map page	283
GPS co-ordinates	S 33° 32′ 18.9″ E 021° 41′ 10.6″
Established	1928
Owner	Calitzdorp Cellar
Cellarmaster	Alwyn Burger
Winemaker	Abraham Pretorius
Viticulturist	Johannes Mellet
First bottled vintage	1970
Area under vines	300 ha
Main varieties	Hanep, Cbard, Chard, Cab Sauv
Red : white ratio	20 : 80
Total bottle production	49 000

Contact Details

Tel	044 213 3301
Email	info@calitzdorpwine.co.za
Web	www.calitzdorpwine.co.za
Tasting days & hours	Mon-Fri & Pub Hols 9-5; Sat 9-1
Tasting fee	Complimentary
Other attractions	Verandah with valley view, Vetplant garden

Personal Tasting Notes

Judges' Comments

Ripe, sweet with pure blackberry and black cherry fruit with a hint of mint.

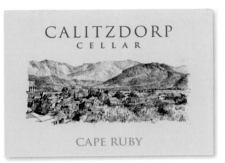

Wine Details

Wine of origin	Calitzdorp	
Alcohol level	18.41%	
Residual Sugar g/L	97.6	
Total Acid g/L	5.5	
pH	3.91	
Closure type	Cork	
Single vineyard	n/a	
Grape varietals	Tour N	Tinta B
Percentage	50%	50%
Irrigated	yes	yes
Farm method	fair	fair
Debut vintage	1990	
Total bottles produced	3 360	
Approx retail price	R 38	

Vinification	Grapes had skin contact in open static drainers for 4 days while it was pumped over and pushed through with a spatula. Fortified with brandy spirits at 11°B.
Oaking	French oak for 6 months.
Maturation	Wine put in old vats for 6 and 12 months.
Ageing potential	8 years

Winemaker Notes

Intensive blackcurrant with leathery spicy aromas. Rich, round, well balanced in mouth. Predominantly Ruby Port full-ripe berries overflow with soft brown chocolate tones and a gentle grip.

Producer Details

Vineyard/Producer	Calitzdorp Cellar
Physical address	Andries Pretorius Street, Calitzdorp
Map page	283
GPS co-ordinates	S 33° 32' 18.9" E 021° 41' 10.6"
Established	1928
Owner	Calitzdorp Cellar
Cellarmaster	Alwyn Burger
Winemaker	Abraham Pretorius
Viticulturist	Johannes Mellet
First bottled vintage	1970
Area under vines	300 ha
Main varieties	Hanep, Cbard, Chard, Cab Sauv
Red : white ratio	20 : 80
Total bottle production	49 000

Contact Details

Tel	044 213 3301
Email	info@calitzdorpwine.co.za
Web	www.calitzdorpwine.co.za
Tasting days & hours	Mon-Fri & Pub Hols 9-5; Sat 9-1
Tasting fee	Complimentary
Other attractions	Verandah with valley view, Vetplant garden

Personal Tasting Notes

Judges' Comments

Lovely ripe cherry and rasberry fruit nose with a sweet palate showing ripe fruit and rooibos tea notes. Lovely varietal character.

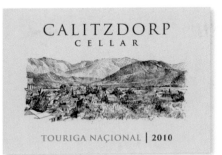

Wine Details

Wine of origin	Calitzdorp
Alcohol level	15%
Residual Sugar g/L	3.5
Total Acid g/L	6
pH	3.4
Closure type	Cork
Single vineyard	Yes
Grape varietals	Tour N
Percentage	100%
Irrigated	yes
Farm method	fair
Debut vintage	2005
Total bottles produced	3 500
Approx retail price	R 32

Vinification	Grapes had skin contact in closed red wine tanks while it was pumped over to get more colour and aroma extraction.
Oaking	French oak barrels for 10 months.
Maturation	As per oaking regime.
Ageing potential	5 years

Winemaker Notes

Sweet liquorice and dark cherry flavours underline this highly accessible table wine. Serve below 20°C. Ideal with roasts, steak or traditional country food like stews.

Producer Details

Vineyard/Producer	Cape Point Vineyards
Physical address	1 Chapman's Peak Drive, Noordhoek
Map page	267
GPS co-ordinates	S 34° 5' 41.85" E 018° 22' 17.28"
Established	1997
Owner	Sybrand Van Der Spuy
Cellarmaster	Duncan Savage
Winemaker	Duncan Savage
Viticulturist	Duncan Savage
First bottled vintage	2000
Area under vines	22 ha
Main varieties	Sauv B, Sem, Chard
Red : white ratio	100% white
Total bottle production	48 000

Contact Details

Tel	021 789 0900
Email	sales@cape-point.com
Web	www.noordhoekvineyards.co.za
Tasting days & hours	Mon-Fri 9-5; Sat 10-5; Sun 10-4
Tasting fee	R 15
Other attractions	Picnic & sundowner site

Personal Tasting Notes

Judges' Comments

Exuberant gooseberry nose. Rich and dense palate. Waxy and layered. Attractive creamy notes with a passion fruit overlay.

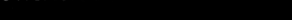

CAPE POINT
V I N E Y A R D S

SAUVIGNON BLANC
RESERVE
2010

WINE OF ORIGIN
CAPE POINT

Wine Details

Wine of origin	Cape Point
Alcohol level	14%
Residual Sugar g/L	2.8
Total Acid g/L	7.3
pH	3.14
Closure type	Cork
Single vineyard	Yes, Noordhoek
Grape varietals	Sauv B
Percentage	100%
Irrigated	yes
Farm method	bio
Debut vintage	2001
Total bottles produced	6 000
Approx retail price	R 155
Vinification	Inoculated and spontaneous ferments. 100% barrel fermented in French oak.
Oaking	French oak for 14 months.
Maturation	As per oaking regime.
Ageing potential	5-10 years

Winemaker Notes

The nose shows delicate floral elements, grapefruit, stone fruit and limes along with subtle wood spice. A rich textured palate all held together by an incredible mineral backbone.

Producer Details

Vineyard/Producer	Capelands Estate
Physical address	3 Old Sir Lowry's Pass Road, Somerset West
Map page	274-275
GPS co-ordinates	S 34° 10' 82.5" E 018° 8' 84.5"
Established	2004
Owner	Capelands Estate
Cellarmaster	Louis Nel
Winemaker	Louis Nel
Viticulturist	Francois Hanekom
First bottled vintage	2010
Area under vines	2.5 ha
Main varieties	Cab Sauv, Malb
Red : white ratio	100% red
Total bottle production	4 000

Contact Details

Tel	021 858 1477
Email	restaurant@capelands.com
Web	www.capelands.com
Tasting days & hours	n/a
Tasting fee	n/a
Other attractions	Restaurant with stunning sea views

Personal Tasting Notes

Judges' Comments

Brooding nose of spice, clove and cassis. Direct fruit on the palate with good punch. Stylish, firm with potential. A hint of eucalypt.

Wine Details

Wine of origin	Stellenbosch	
Alcohol level	14.5%	
Residual Sugar g/L	3	
Total Acid g/L	4.8	
pH	3.5	
Closure type	Cork	
Single vineyard	n/a	
Grape varietals	Cab Sauv	Malb
Percentage	85%	15%
Irrigated	no	n/a
Farm method	n/a	n/a
Debut vintage	2010	
Total bottles produced	4 000	
Approx retail price	R 150	
Vinification	Traditional vinification.	
Oaking	Unoaked.	
Maturation	220L 2nd and 3rd fill barrels for 12 to 14 months.	
Ageing potential	10 years +	

Winemaker Notes

Wild berries, ripe plum, cassis, luscious cedar, liquorice, black olive flavors abound on the nose. Red berries and plum follow through onto the palate and complement the soft chewy tannins.

Producer Details

Vineyard/Producer	Cederberg Private Cellar
Physical address	Dwarsrivier Farm, Cederberg
Map page	282
GPS co-ordinates	S 32° 30′ 12.8″ E 019° 15′ 27.7″
Established	1973
Owner	David & Ernst Nieuwoudt
Cellarmaster	David Nieuwoudt
Winemaker	David Nieuwoudt
Viticulturist	Ernst Nieuwoudt
First bottled vintage	1977
Area under vines	53 ha
Main varieties	Sauv B, Chen Bl, Bukettraube, Cab Sauv
Red : white ratio	50 : 50
Total bottle production	300 000

Contact Details

Tel	027 482 2827
Email	jaco@cederbergwine.com
Web	www.cederbergwine.com
Tasting days & hours	Mon-Sat 8-12 & 2-4.30; Pub Hols 9-11.30 & 4-5.30
Tasting fee	R 20
Other attractions	Accom, observatory

Personal Tasting Notes

Judges' Comments

Serious wine showing concentrated fruit of dark plum, liquorice, peppercorns. Sturdy and yet attractive. Supported by firm tannins and a silky long aftertaste.

CEDERBERG
SOUTH AFRICA

middingvanis cederbergvanis

CABERNET SAUVIGNON 2009

Wine Details

Wine of origin	Cederberg
Alcohol level	14.41%
Residual Sugar g/L	2.7
Total Acid g/L	6
pH	3.79
Closure type	Cork
Single vineyard	n/a
Grape varietals	Cab Sauv
Percentage	100%
Irrigated	yes
Farm method	n/a
Debut vintage	1977
Total bottles produced	24 408
Approx retail price	R 125

Vinification	Berries crushed, cold maceration for 4 days. Inoculate yeast. Pump overs every 4 hours. Extended skin contact for 21 days. Malolactic fermentation in barrels.
Oaking	14 months in medium toast French oak, Nevers and Allier.
Maturation	14 months maturation in French oak barrels. 70% 1st fill and 30% 2nd fill barrels.
Ageing potential	4-8 years

Winemaker Notes

Concentrated dark fruits of blackcurrant and cassis laced with a subtle mint undertone. 14 months maturation in French oak lends a hint of tobacco leaf and adds an intricate smoky element.

Producer Details

Vineyard/Producer	Cederberg Private Cellar
Physical address	Dwarsrivier Farm, Cederberg
Map page	282
GPS co-ordinates	S 32° 30' 12.8" E 019° 15' 27.7"
Established	1973
Owner	David & Ernst Nieuwoudt
Cellarmaster	David Nieuwoudt
Winemaker	David Nieuwoudt
Viticulturist	Ernst Nieuwoudt
First bottled vintage	1977
Area under vines	53 ha
Main varieties	Sauv B, Chen Bl, Bukettraube, Cab Sauv
Red : white ratio	50 : 50
Total bottle production	300 000

Contact Details

Tel	027 482 2827
Email	jaco@cederbergwine.com
Web	www.cederbergwine.com
Tasting days & hours	Mon-Sat 8-12 & 2-4.30;
	Pub Hols 9-11.30 & 4-5.30
Tasting fee	R 20
Other attractions	Accom, observatory

Personal Tasting Notes

Judges' Comments

Elegant wine with ripe blackberry, rasberry and blackcurrants. Exuberant but well-handled tight, grained, cedary oak.

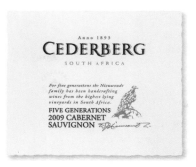

Wine Details

Wine of origin	Cederberg
Alcohol level	14.26%
Residual Sugar g/L	2
Total Acid g/L	6.2
pH	3.75
Closure type	Cork
Single vineyard	n/a
Grape varietals	Cab Sauv
Percentage	100%
Irrigated	yes
Farm method	n/a
Debut vintage	2000
Total bottles produced	3 469
Approx retail price	R 300

Vinification	Berries crushed, cold maceration 4 days. Inoculate yeast. Pump overs every 6 hours. Extended skin contact 21 days. Malolactic fermentation in barrels. Press.
Oaking	18 months in French oak, Nevers and Allier.
Maturation	18 months maturation in 100% new French oak from 12 selected barrels.
Ageing potential	5-12 years

Winemaker Notes

18 months in new French oak intensifies the rich aromas of blackcurrant and cassis, layered with decadent dark chocolate and cherry tobacco. Plush velvety finish leaves one wanting more.

Producer Details

Vineyard/Producer	Cederberg Private Cellar
Physical address	Dwarsrivier Farm, Cederberg
Map page	282
GPS co-ordinates	S 32° 30' 12.8" E 019° 15' 27.7"
Established	1973
Owner	David & Ernst Nieuwoudt
Cellarmaster	David Nieuwoudt
Winemaker	David Nieuwoudt
Viticulturist	Ernst Nieuwoudt
First bottled vintage	1977
Area under vines	53 ha
Main varieties	Sauv B, Chen Bl, Bukettraube, Cab Sauv
Red : white ratio	50 : 50
Total bottle production	300 000

Contact Details

Tel	027 482 2827
Email	jaco@cederbergwine.com
Web	www.cederbergwine.com
Tasting days & hours	Mon-Sat 8-12 & 2-4.30;
	Pub Hols 9-11.30 & 4-5.30
Tasting fee	R 20
Other attractions	Accom, observatory

Personal Tasting Notes

Judges' Comments

Cool grassy, green pea and lime aromas. Cool, lemongrass and citrus flavours drive a rounded and lively palate.

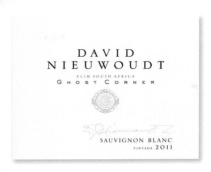

Wine Details

Wine of origin	Elim
Alcohol level	13.24%
Residual Sugar g/L	2.6
Total Acid g/L	7
pH	3.37
Closure type	Screw cap
Single vineyard	n/a
Grape varietals	Sauv B
Percentage	100%
Irrigated	yes
Farm method	n/a
Debut vintage	2008
Total bottles produced	15 311
Approx retail price	R 165
Vinification	Reductive style, cold crush 8ºC, skin contact for 8 hours. Light pressing, only free run juice used. Settle for 2 days at 10ºC. Fermentation 21 days at 12ºC.
Oaking	Unoaked.
Maturation	5 months lees contact. Tank battonage once a week.
Ageing potential	2-4 years

Winemaker Notes

Layers of green figs and gooseberries with a touch of grapefruit, fynbos and a steely minerality, a reflection of the cool climate terroir of Elim where the grapes are sourced.

Producer Details

Vineyard/Producer	Cederberg Private Cellar
Physical address	Dwarsrivier Farm, Cederberg
Map page	282
GPS co-ordinates	S 32° 30' 12.8" E 019° 15' 27.7"
Established	1973
Owner	David & Ernst Nieuwoudt
Cellarmaster	David Nieuwoudt
Winemaker	David Nieuwoudt
Viticulturist	Ernst Nieuwoudt
First bottled vintage	1977
Area under vines	53 ha
Main varieties	Sauv B, Chen Bl, Bukettraube, Cab Sauv
Red : white ratio	50 : 50
Total bottle production	300 000

Contact Details

Tel	027 482 2827
Email	jaco@cederbergwine.com
Web	www.cederbergwine.com
Tasting days & hours	Mon-Sat 8-12 & 2-4.30; Pub Hols 9-11.30 & 4-5.30
Tasting fee	R 20
Other attractions	Accom, observatory

Personal Tasting Notes

Judges' Comments

Dense, rich and spicy with notes of herbs, charred crème brûlée character. Rich blackberry and plum fruit meshing well with the oak.

CEDERBERG
SOUTH AFRICA

milddergrouw cedarbergmaste

MERLOT · SHIRAZ 2009

Wine Details

Wine of origin	Cederberg
Alcohol level	14.95%
Residual Sugar g/L	3.5
Total Acid g/L	5.5
pH	3.66
Closure type	Cork
Single vineyard	n/a
Grape varietals	Shiraz
Percentage	100%
Irrigated	yes
Farm method	n/a
Debut vintage	2001
Total bottles produced	29 320
Approx retail price	R 140

Vinification	Berries crushed. Cold maceration 4 days. Inoculate yeast. Pump overs every 6 hours. Extended skin contact 21 days. Light press. MLF in barrels.
Oaking	15 months in medium toast French oak, Nevers and Allier, and American oak.
Maturation	15 months maturation in 95% French oak and 5% American oak. 70% 1st fill and 30% 2nd fill barrels.
Ageing potential	4-8 years

Winemaker Notes

Expect intense mulberry flavours layered with roasted coffee beans, dark chocolate and spice. Well-structured wine with a lingering velvet finish. Will age superbly in the next 4-8 years.

Producer Details

Vineyard/Producer	Van Loveren
Physical address	R317, between Robertson & Bonnievale
Map page	280
GPS co-ordinates	S 33° 52′ 31.3″ E 020° 0′ 9.1″
Established	1937
Owner	Retief Brothers
Cellarmaster	Bussell Retief
Winemaker	Danelle van Rensburg
Viticulturist	Neil Retief
First bottled vintage	1980
Area under vines	400 ha
Main varieties	Sauv B, Cab Sauv, Shiraz, Chard, Sem, Merl
Red : white ratio	50 : 50
Total bottle production	12 000 000

Contact Details

Tel	023 615 1505
Email	winemaker@vanloveren.co.za
Web	www.vanloveren.co.za
Tasting days & hours	Mon-Fri 8.30-5; Sat 9:30-1; Sun 11-2
Tasting fee	Complimentary
Other attractions	n/a

Personal Tasting Notes

Judges' Comments

Intriguing meaty, olive nose with sweet fruit. Lovely blackberry and cherry fruit. Stylish and ripe. Classy.

Wine Details

Wine of origin	Western Cape	
Alcohol level	13.91%	
Residual Sugar g/L	2.8	
Total Acid g/L	5.4	
pH	3.68	
Closure type	Cork	
Single vineyard	n/a	
Grape varietals	Shiraz	Viog
Percentage	93%	7%
Irrigated	yes	yes
Farm method	n/a	n/a
Debut vintage	2009	
Total bottles produced	2 922	
Approx retail price	R 105	

Vinification	Not specified
Oaking	French and American oak for 14 months.
Maturation	100% new 300L barrels, 10% American, 90% French oak.
Ageing potential	5 years

Winemaker Notes

A full-bodied, well-structed showcase Shiraz. The wine was matured in new French oak barrels and has a light peppery scent of ripe berries, perfume and spice and will gain complexity.

Producer Details

Vineyard/Producer	Dalla Cia
Physical address	7A Lower Dorp Street, Bosman's Crossing, Stellenbosch
Map page	268-269
GPS co-ordinates	S 33° 56' 25.8" E 018° 50' 50.1"
Established	2004
Owner	Giorgio Dalla Cia
Cellarmaster	Giorgio Dalla Cia
Winemaker	Giorgio Dalla Cia
Viticulturist	n/a
First bottled vintage	2002
Area under vines	n/a
Main varieties	Sauv B, Chard, Cab Sauv, Cab Fr, Merl, Pet V
Red : white ratio	70 : 30
Total bottle production	84 000

Contact Details

Tel	021 888 4120
Email	george@dallacia.com
Web	www.dallacia.com
Tasting days & hours	Mon-Sat 10-5.30; Sun & Pub Hols closed
Tasting fee	Various (waived upon purchase)
Other attractions	Grappa distillery tours

Personal Tasting Notes

Judges' Comments

Gravelly and dark with minty cassis fruit and some coffee-bean notes. It's well judged, fresh and quite elegant.

GIORGIO

2007

DALLA CIA

Wine Details

Wine of origin	Stellenbosch		
Alcohol level	14.5%		
Residual Sugar g/L	2.41		
Total Acid g/L	6.26		
pH	3.57		
Closure type	Cork		
Single vineyard	n/a		
Grape varietals	Cab Sauv	Cab Fr	Pet V
Percentage	70%	20%	10%
Irrigated	yes	yes	yes
Farm method	n/a	n/a	n/a
Debut vintage	2002		
Total bottles produced	16 000		
Approx retail price	R 210		

Vinification	Fermented dry with selected yeast. Malolactic fermentation.
Oaking	French oak for 18 months.
Maturation	Matured in 70% new and 30% 2nd fill French oak barrels for 18 months.
Ageing potential	10 years +

Winemaker Notes

Hints of coffee beans, vanilla, tobacco leaf and spiced cedarwood bouquet. The mouthfeel is opulent with a generous lingering aftertaste. This wine has great ageing potential.

Producer Details

Vineyard/Producer	Diemersdal Wine Estate
Physical address	Koeberg Road, M58, Durbanville
Map page	270
GPS co-ordinates	S 33° 48' 06" E 018° 52' 15"
Established	1698
Owner	M M Louw
Cellarmaster	n/a
Winemaker	Thys Louw
Viticulturist	Div van Niekerk
First bottled vintage	1976
Area under vines	182 ha
Main varieties	Sauv B, Cab Sauv, Ptage, Shiraz
Red : white ratio	37 : 63
Total bottle production	67 443

Contact Details

Tel	021 976 3361
Email	info@diemersdal.co.za
Web	www.diemersdal.co.za
Tasting days & hours	Mon-Fri 9-5; Sat 9-3
Tasting fee	Complimentary
Other attractions	n/a

Personal Tasting Notes

Judges' Comments

Lively, ginger notes with lime and exotic fruits, complemented by good use of oak adding a creamy note. Commendably full mid-palate with pithy, fresh acidity.

Six generations of MM Louw

Est.1698 | DIEMERSDAL | Sauvignon Blanc
ESTATE WINE OF ORIGIN DURBANVILLE | unfiltered, barrel fermented
WINE OF SOUTH AFRICA | 2011

Wine Details

Wine of origin	Durbanville
Alcohol level	13.98%
Residual Sugar g/L	1.7
Total Acid g/L	7.5
pH	3.35
Closure type	Cork & synthetic
Single vineyard	n/a
Grape varietals	Sauv B
Percentage	100%
Irrigated	no
Farm method	n/a
Debut vintage	2007
Total bottles produced	1 275
Approx retail price	R 165
Vinification	Hand harvested, fermented with natural yeast in 500L new French oak barrels.
Oaking	French oak for 10 months.
Maturation	10 months in French oak. New wood component is 20%. Transferred to tank in Jan 2011, prepared for bottling in Apr 2011.
Ageing potential	2-8 years

Winemaker Notes

Full, rich mouthfeel with a long finish. Flavours of fynbos, asparagus and tropical fruit are underpinned by a core of minerality and complex fruit and vanilla flavours.

Producer Details

Vineyard/Producer	Doolhof Wine Estate
Physical address	Bovlei Road, Wellington
Map page	272-273
GPS co-ordinates	S 33° 37' 35.6" E 019° 4' 58.7"
Established	2004
Owner	D Kerrison
Cellarmaster	n/a
Winemaker	Friedrich Kuhn
Viticulturist	Hendrik Laubscher
First bottled vintage	2005
Area under vines	38.5 ha
Main varieties	Malb, Merl, Ptage, Cab Fr, Pet V
Red : white ratio	73% red, 26% white, 1% rosé
Total bottle production	60 000-70 000

Contact Details

Tel	021 873 6911
Email	wine@doolhof.com
Web	www.doolhof.com
Tasting days & hours	Mon-Sun 8-5
Tasting fee	R 20 for 5 wines
Other attractions	River & vineyard walks

Personal Tasting Notes

Judges' Comments

Minty, eucalyptus nose with lovely sweet plums and berry fruits.
Notes of blackcurrant and mint with a sappy underbelly.

Wine Details

Wine of origin	Wellington
Alcohol level	14.5%
Residual Sugar g/L	3.1
Total Acid g/L	5.6
pH	3.54
Closure type	Cork
Single vineyard	n/a
Grape varietals	Malb
Percentage	100%
Irrigated	n/a
Farm method	n/a
Debut vintage	Not specified
Total bottles produced	5 075
Approx retail price	R 115
Vinification	Cold soaked for 3 days. Pump overs 3 x daily. Extended maturation on skins after fermentation for 14 days. Malolactic fermentation done in tanks after pressing.
Oaking	French oak for 14 months.
Maturation	Matured in 225L French oak barrels for 14 months. Best barrels selected and final blend done prior to bottling.
Ageing potential	8 years

Winemaker Notes

Intense purple. Blackberries, eucalyptus to the fore, fresh mint, vanilla and touch of sandalwood. Palate shows freshness, youth, juicy fruit. Good structure, soft well-integrated tannins.

Producer Details

Vineyard/Producer	Du Toit Family Wines
Physical address	Driehoek Farm, Cederberg
Map page	282
GPS co-ordinates	S 32° 26′ 34.4″Đ E 019° 11′ 24.32″
Established	2009
Owner	Charl du Toit
Cellarmaster	David Nieuwoudt
Winemaker	David Nieuwoudt
Viticulturist	Dawie Burger & Hennie Spamer with David Nieuwoudt
First bottled vintage	2009
Area under vines	4.5 ha
Main varieties	Sauv B, Shiraz, Pinot
Red : white ratio	50 : 50
Total bottle production	15 000

Contact Details

Tel	027 482 2827
Email	jaco@cederbergwine.com
Web	www.cederberg-accommodation.co.za
Tasting days	n/a
Tasting fee	n/a
Attractions	Gift shop, BYO picnic, hiking, mountain biking

Personal Tasting Notes

Judges' Comments

Taut with polished mahogany, boot polish and cloves as well as bright berry fruits. Very appealing and spicy.

DU TOIT FAMILIE
DRIEHOEK
Cederberg

2010 SHIRAZ

WYNE VAN DIE CEDERBERG
SUID-AFRIKA

Wine Details

Wine of origin	Cederberg
Alcohol level	14.94%
Residual Sugar g/L	4.1
Total Acid g/L	6.4
pH	3.35
Closure type	Cork
Single vineyard	n/a
Grape varietals	Shiraz
Percentage	100%
Irrigated	yes
Farm method	n/a
Debut vintage	2009
Total bottles produced	4 296
Approx retail price	R 150
Vinification	Cold maceration for 4 days, inoculate yeast, pump overs every 6 hours, extended skin contact for 21 days, malolactic fermentation in new French oak barrels.
Oaking	French oak for 15 months.
Maturation	15 months maturation in French oak. 70% 1st fill and 30% 2nd fill barrels.
Ageing potential	5-8 years

Winemaker Notes

Rich concentrated nose of ripe black fruits with sweet spice and good oak structure. Full, rounded palate, smooth ripe tannins and fresh acidity.

Producer Details

Vineyard/Producer	Eenzaamheid
Physical address	Corner of R312 & Eenzaamheid Road, Agter-Paarl
Map page	272-273
GPS co-ordinates	n/a
Established	1693
Owner	Christo Briers-Louw
Cellarmaster	Janno Briers-Louw
Winemaker	Janno Briers-Louw
Viticulturist	Andre Coetzee
First bottled vintage	2010
Area under vines	380 ha
Main varieties	Chen Bl, Shiraz, Ptage, Mourv, Cins, Cab Sauv
Red : white ratio	60 : 40
Total bottle production	4 500

Contact Details

Tel	082 493 9930
Email	wine@eenzaamheid1.co.za
Web	n/a
Tasting days & hours	By appointment
Tasting fee	Complimentary
Other attractions	Newly renovated historic building dating to 1688

Personal Tasting Notes

Judges' Comments

Waxy green apples with some vanilla pod as well as broad, nutty fruit. Honeyed and a bit spicy with nice precision.

Wine Details

Wine of origin	Paarl
Alcohol level	13.8%
Residual Sugar g/L	1.8
Total Acid g/L	6.5
pH	3.46
Closure type	Cork
Single vineyard	n/a
Grape varietals	Chen Bl
Percentage	100%
Irrigated	no
Farm method	n/a
Debut vintage	2011
Total bottles produced	750
Approx retail price	R 120

Vinification	Barrel fermented and aged sur lie in French oak barrels for 11 months with regular stirring of the lees. No malolactic fermentation.
Oaking	French oak for 11 months.
Maturation	Aged sur lie in French oak barrels for 11 months with regular stirring of the lees.
Ageing potential	3-5 years

Winemaker Notes

A full-bodied wine with a very obvious tropical fruit character supported by oaky aromas. Fresh acidity.

Producer Details

Vineyard/Producer	Eikendal Vineyards
Physical address	R44, Stellenbosch
Map page	274-275
GPS co-ordinates	S 34° 0' 46.7" E 018° 49' 24.5"
Established	1981
Owner	Substantia AG
Cellarmaster	Nico Grobler
Winemaker	Nico Grobler
Viticulturist	Nico Grobler
First bottled vintage	1984
Area under vines	56 ha
Main varieties	Chard, Merl, Cab Fr, Cab Sauv
Red : white ratio	60 : 40
Total bottle production	250 000

Contact Details

Tel	021 855 1422
Email	nico@eikendal.co.za
Web	www.eikendal.com
Tasting days & hours	Mon-Sun 9.30-4.30
Tasting fee	R 25
Other attractions	Restaurant, fly fishing, lodge

Personal Tasting Notes

Judges' Comments

Noted menthol, creamy texture. This is a lighter example showing great finesse and well-integrated oak.

Wine Details

Wine of origin	Stellenbosch
Alcohol level	14.5%
Residual Sugar g/L	2
Total Acid g/L	6
pH	3.45
Closure type	Cork
Single vineyard	n/a
Grape varietals	Cab Sauv
Percentage	100%
Irrigated	yes
Farm method	n/a
Debut vintage	1984
Total bottles produced	9 000
Approx retail price	R 85
Vinification	Pre-soaking for 5-7 days at 5°C. Slow long fermentation, 2 punch downs a day. Pressed when dry.
Oaking	300L French oak for 15 months.
Maturation	20% new oak. Blended and bottled.
Ageing potential	8-14 years

Winemaker Notes

Shows sense of place. Typical Helderberg fruit, black cherry, pastel, lead pencil and shavings. Tightness with almost mineral fresh tannin. Beautiful integration and balance.

Producer Details

Vineyard/Producer	Elgin Heights
Physical address	Smarag Farm, Box 58, Elgin
Map page	
GPS co-ordinates	S 34° 13' 18.34" E 019° 4' 41.83"
Established	1999
Owner	R.J. Joubert
Cellarmaster	n/a
Winemaker	Andries Burger, Kobie Viljoen & Corne Marais
Viticulturist	D.D. Joubert
First bottled vintage	2007
Area under vines	65 ha
Main varieties	Sauv B, Chard, Viog, Cab Sauv, Merl, Shiraz
Red : white ratio	45 : 55
Total bottle production	24 000

Contact Details

Tel	083 275 1535
Email	mwddj@mweb.co.za
Web	www.elginheights.co.za
Tasting days & hours	n/a
Tasting fee	n/a
Other attractions	n/a

Personal Tasting Notes

Judges' Comments

Smooth blackberry and rasberry jam with some crushed granite notes and a hint of mint. Supple, smooth and well defined.

Wine Details

Wine of origin	Elgin
Alcohol level	14%
Residual Sugar g/L	3.19
Total Acid g/L	5.6
pH	3.45
Closure type	Cork
Single vineyard	n/a
Grape varietals	Shiraz
Percentage	100%
Irrigated	yes
Farm method	n/a
Debut vintage	2009
Total bottles produced	6 500
Approx retail price	R 90

Vinification	Grapes hand sorted, cold soaked.
Oaking	French and American oak for 14 months.
Maturation	Matured in the barrel and 2 years in bottle.
Ageing potential	5 years +

Winemaker Notes

'Quality engraved' by good viticultural practices, passion and attention to detail on all levels of the process.

ELGIN VINTNERS

Producer Details

Vineyard/Producer	Elgin Vintners
Physical address	Morningstar Farm, Oudebrug Road, Elgin
Map page	278
GPS co-ordinates	S 34° 10' 4.9" E 019° 2' 1.3"
Established	2003
Owner	J Rawbone-Viljoen, P Wallace, A Moodie & M Hahn
Cellarmaster	Various
Winemaker	Various
Viticulturist	Paul Wallace
First bottled vintage	2003
Area under vines	101 ha
Main varieties	Sauv B, Chard, Viog, Sem, Pinot, Shiraz, Merl
Red : white ratio	60 : 40
Total bottle production	15 000

Contact Details

Tel	021 859 2779
Email	elginvintner@mweb.co.za
Web	www.elginvintners.co.za
Tasting days & hours	By appointment
Tasting fee	Complimentary
Other attractions	Tastings conducted in heart of cellar

Personal Tasting Notes

Judges' Comments

Very herbal edge to the wine – combines greenness with ripe, lush fruit.

Wine Details

Wine of origin	Elgin
Alcohol level	15%
Residual Sugar g/L	1.6
Total Acid g/L	5.6
pH	3.71
Closure type	Synthetic
Single vineyard	n/a
Grape varietals	Shiraz
Percentage	100%
Irrigated	yes
Farm method	n/a
Debut vintage	2005
Total bottles produced	9 800
Approx retail price	R 99
Vinification	Harvested on 2 Apr 2008 and vinified at Luddite by Niels Verburg.
Oaking	Mostly 225L French oak barrels for 14 months.
Maturation	Matured in 225L French oak for 20 months. New wood component was 25%. Bottled on 16 Feb 2010.
Ageing potential	At least 3-5 years

Winemaker Notes

Vibrant, dark garnet colour. Rich and decadent entry of toasty spice and dark plummy fruit. Palate yields full, broad, dark fruits backed by hints of dark chocolate and spice.

Producer Details

Vineyard/Producer	Ernie Els Wines
Physical address	Annandale Road, Stellenbosch
Map page	268-269
GPS co-ordinates	S 34° 0' 52.8" E 018° 50' 53.5"
Established	1999
Owner	Ernie Els
Cellarmaster	Louis Strydom
Winemaker	Louis Strydom
Viticulturist	Charl van Reenen
First bottled vintage	2000
Area under vines	51 ha
Main varieties	Cab Sauv, Merl, Shiraz
Red : white ratio	100% red
Total bottle production	250 000

Contact Details

Tel	021 881 3588
Email	info@ernieelswines.com
Web	www.ernieelswines.com
Tasting days & hours	Mon-Sat 9-5
Tasting fee	R 30 (selective tasting), R 60 (portfolio tasting)
Other attractions	Light lunches, cellar visits, trophy room

Personal Tasting Notes

Judges' Comments

Crushed cranberries, red cherry, floral notes. Meat and game flavours on palate. Layered and silky tannins, well structured, attractive, well flavoured.

Wine Details

Wine of origin	Stellenbosch					
Alcohol level	14%					
Residual Sugar g/L	3					
Total Acid g/L	6.3					
pH	3.64					
Closure type	Cork					
Single vineyard	n/a					
Grape varietals	Shiraz	Cab Sauv	Gren	Mourv	Cins	Viog
Percentage	67%	16%	4%	4%	6%	3%
Irrigated	yes	yes	yes	yes	yes	yes
Farm method	n/a	n/a	n/a	n/a	n/a	n/a
Debut vintage	2001					
Total bottles produced	28 282					
Approx retail price	R 120					

Vinification	Harvest at 25° balling, fermentation in stainless steel tanks.
Oaking	French and American oak for 12 months.
Maturation	12 months, 80% French oak, 20% American oak.
Ageing potential	5 years

Winemaker Notes

An alluring kaleidoscope of black fruits, Christmas cake, liquorice and cinnamon tempt your nose, leading to a dense and full-bodied palate.

Producer Details

Vineyard/Producer	Ernie Els Wines
Physical address	Annandale Road, Stellenbosch
Map page	268-269
GPS co-ordinates	S 34° 0′ 52.8″ E 018° 50′ 53.5″
Established	1999
Owner	Ernie Els
Cellarmaster	Louis Strydom
Winemaker	Louis Strydom
Viticulturist	Charl van Reenen
First bottled vintage	2000
Area under vines	51 ha
Main varieties	Cab Sauv, Merl, Shiraz
Red : white ratio	100% red
Total bottle production	250 000

Contact Details

Tel	021 881 3588
Email	info@ernieelswines.com
Web	www.ernieelswines.com
Tasting days & hours	Mon-Sat 9-5
Tasting fee	R 30 (selective), R 60 (portfolio)
Other attractions	Light lunches, cellar visits, trophy room

Personal Tasting Notes

Judges' Comments

Distinctive aromatic nose with apricot notes from the Viognier working well with the smooth sweet damson and plum notes.

Wine Details

Wine of origin	Stellenbosch	
Alcohol level	14%	
Residual Sugar g/L	3.2	
Total Acid g/L	6.3	
pH	3.7	
Closure type	Cork	
Single vineyard	n/a	
Grape varietals	Shiraz	Viog
Percentage	94%	6%
Irrigated	yes	yes
Farm method	n/a	n/a
Debut vintage	2011	
Total bottles produced	6 750	
Approx retail price	R 210	

Vinification	Harvest at 25° balling, fermentation in stainless steel tanks.
Oaking	French and American oak for 18 months.
Maturation	18 months, 70% French oak, 30% American oak.
Ageing potential	5-10 years

Winemaker Notes

A dense, pitch-black core with a vivid purple hue. Intense blueberries, pepper ham and warm toast flavors, crescendos in a sweet spice and wood-smoke ensemble.

Producer Details

Vineyard/Producer	Ernie Els Wines
Physical address	Annandale Road, Stellenbosch
Map page	268-269
GPS co-ordinates	S 34° 0' 52.8" E 018° 50' 53.5"
Established	1999
Owner	Ernie Els
Cellarmaster	Louis Strydom
Winemaker	Louis Strydom
Viticulturist	Charl van Reenen
First bottled vintage	2000
Area under vines	51 ha
Main varieties	Cab Sauv, Merl, Shiraz
Red : white ratio	100% red
Total bottle production	250 000

Contact Details

Tel	021 881 3588
Email	info@ernieelswines.com
Web	www.ernieelswines.com
Tasting days & hours	Mon-Sat 9-5
Tasting fee	R 30 (selective tasting)
	R 60 (portfolio tasting)
Other attractions	Light lunches, cellar visits, trophy room

Personal Tasting Notes

Judges' Comments

Ripe, exotic, aromatic note with sweet black fruits leading to a compact palate with a hint of coffee and nice ripe fruit. Fine tannins.

Wine Details

Wine of origin	Stellenbosch				
Alcohol level	14.5%				
Residual Sugar g/L	3				
Total Acid g/L	6.1				
pH	3.81				
Closure type	Cork				
Single vineyard	n/a				
Grape varietals	Cab Sauv	Merl	Pet V	Malb	Cab Fr
Percentage	57%	28%	5%	5%	5%
Irrigated	yes	yes	yes	yes	yes
Farm method	n/a	n/a	n/a	n/a	n/a
Debut vintage	2009				
Total bottles produced	6 800				
Approx retail price	R 550				

Vinification	Harvest at 25° balling, fermentation in stainless steel tanks.
Oaking	French oak for 18 months.
Maturation	Aged for 18 months, 300L French oak barrels, 100% new.
Ageing potential	5-10 years

Winemaker Notes

Full bodied. Large Cab Sauv component dominates with rich blackcurrants, whilst the other 4 Bordeaux varieties contribute with exotic hints of mint, pencil shavings, dark olive and rosemary.

Producer Details

Vineyard/Producer	Glenwood
Physical address	Robertsvlei Road, Franschhoek
Map page	271
GPS co-ordinates	S 33° 54' 94.9" E 019° 04' 97.8"
Established	1989
Owner	AG Wood
Cellarmaster	DP Burger
Winemaker	DP Burger
Viticulturist	DP Burger
First bottled vintage	2002
Area under vines	30 ha
Main varieties	Chard
Red : white ratio	50 : 50
Total bottle production	98 000

Contact Details

Tel	021 876 2044
Email	info@glenwoodvineyards.co.za
Web	www.glenwoodvineyards.co.za
Tasting days & hours	Mon-Fri 11-4; Sat & Sun 11-3
Tasting fee	R 30 (tasting),
	R 50 (cellar tour & tasting)
Other attractions	Pristine surroundings
	of the farm, BYO picnics

Personal Tasting Notes

Judges' Comments

Oaky nose, toasty, rich, spicy and buttery. Rounded, rich, oak-driven palate with soft rich fruit.

Wine Details

Wine of origin	Franschhoek
Alcohol level	13.56%
Residual Sugar g/L	1.3
Total Acid g/L	4.7
pH	3.65
Closure type	Cork
Single vineyard	n/a
Grape varietals	Chard
Percentage	100%
Irrigated	yes
Farm method	n/a
Debut vintage	2000
Total bottles produced	4 750
Approx retail price	R 95
Vinification	Whole bunch pressed. 100% barrel fermented using all wild yeast. Matured 12 months in all new 225L French oak barrels. 100% natural malolactic fermentation.
Oaking	12 months in all new 225L French oak barrels.
Maturation	As per oaking regime.
Ageing potential	4-6 years

Winemaker Notes

Fantastic fruit and oak integration. Well balanced with a full, rich, creamy mouthfeel of almonds and vanilla, a lingering aftertaste of smoky peach and citrus fruit. Fantastic food wine.

Producer Details

Vineyard/Producer	Groot Constantia
Physical address	Groot Constantia Road, Constantia
Map page	267
GPS co-ordinates	S 34° 01' 37.03" E 018° 25' 28.84"
Established	1685
Owner	Groot Constantia Trust NPC
Cellarmaster	n/a
Winemaker	Boela Gerber
Viticulturist	Floricius Beukes
First bottled vintage	1688
Area under vines	90 ha
Main varieties	Sauv B, Sem, Chard, Shiraz, Merl, Malb, Musc
Red : white ratio	70 : 30
Total bottle production	500 000

Contact Details

Tel	021 794 5128
Email	enquiries@grootconstantia.co.za
Web	www.grootconstantia.co.za
Tasting days & hours	Mon-Fri 9-6 (summer), 9-5 (winter)
Tasting fee	R 33 (tasting), R 38 (cellar tour & tasting),
Other attractions	Jonkershuis & Simon's restaurants, Manor House

Personal Tasting Notes

Judges' Comments

Sweet, slightly meaty open berry fruits. Quite sleek and polished with supple fruit and a hint of roast meat.

Wine Details

Wine of origin	Constantia			
Alcohol level	14.5%			
Residual Sugar g/L	1.3			
Total Acid g/L	5.8			
pH	3.65			
Closure type	Cork			
Single vineyard	n/a			
Grape varietals	Cab Sauv	Cab Fr	Merl	Malb
Percentage	32%	33%	28%	7%
Irrigated	yes	yes	yes	yes
Farm method	n/a	n/a	n/a	n/a
Debut vintage	2010			
Total bottles produced	27 477			
Approx retail price	R 240			

Vinification	Grapes earmarked for this blend were treated with special care. Picked at 24-25° balling. During 1st half of fermentation, wine pumped over every 4 hours.
Oaking	New French oak for 15 months.
Maturation	15 months in 225L new French oak vats.
Ageing potential	10-15 years

Winemaker Notes

Deep intense red colour. Many ripe rich flavours on the nose, black cherries, plums, blackcurrant and hints of chocolate and cigar box. These rich flavours follow through on the palate.

Producer Details

Vineyard/Producer	Groot Constantia
Physical address	Groot Constantia Road, Constantia
Map page	267
GPS co-ordinates	S 34° 01' 37.03" E 018° 25' 28.84"
Established	1685
Owner	Groot Constantia Trust NPC
Cellarmaster	n/a
Winemaker	Boela Gerber
Viticulturist	Floricius Beukes
First bottled vintage	1688
Area under vines	90 ha
Main varieties	Sauv B, Sem, Chard, Shiraz, Merl, Malb, Musc
Red : white ratio	70 : 30
Total bottle production	500 000

Contact Details

Tel	021 794 5128
Email	enquiries@grootconstantia.co.za
Web	www.grootconstantia.co.za
Tasting days & hours	Mon-Fri 9-6 (summer), 9-5 (winter)
Tasting fee	R 33 (tasting), R 38 (cellar tour & tasting)
Other attractions	Jonkershuis & Simon's restaurants, Manor House

Personal Tasting Notes

Judges' Comments

*Restrained, tight mineral with orange zest and Galia melon –
excellent example of cool climate expression with pithy texture,
savoury characters and long distinct finish.*

Wine Details

Wine of origin	Constantia	
Alcohol level	13.39%	
Residual Sugar g/L	2.1	
Total Acid g/L	2.4	
pH	3.44	
Closure type	Cork	
Single vineyard	n/a	
Grape varietals	Sem	Sauv B
Percentage	87%	13%
Irrigated	yes	yes
Farm method	n/a	n/a
Debut vintage	2009	
Total bottles produced	3 998	
Approx retail price	R 150	

Vinification	Grapes hand picked and vinified separately in 40% new oak and 60% 2nd and 3rd fill.
Oaking	French oak for 9 months.
Maturation	Matured on its lees for 9 months before bottling. Stirring of lees before bottling added richness to the wine's palate.
Ageing potential	10 years

Winemaker Notes

Pale straw colour with a lime tint. A lot of upfront minerality, delicate orange blossom and almond flavours. Time in the glass shows green pepper, subtle hints of ripe summer fruit flavour.

Producer Details

Vineyard/Producer	Hamilton Russell Vineyards
Physical address	R320, Hemel-en-Aarde Valley, Hermanus
Map page	278
GPS co-ordinates	S 34° 24' 16.3" E 019° 13' 15"
Established	1975
Owner	Anthony Hamilton Russell
Cellarmaster	n/a
Winemaker	Hannes Storm
Viticulturist	Johan Montgomery
First bottled vintage	1981
Area under vines	52 ha
Main varieties	Pinot, Chard
Red : white ratio	50 : 50
Total bottle production	138 384

Contact Details

Tel	028 312 3595
Email	talitahrv@hermanus.co.za
Web	www.hamiltonrussellvineyards.co.za
Tasting days & hours	Mon-Fri 9-5; Sat 9-1
Tasting fee	Complimentary; groups by appointment
Attractions	Estate olive oil & fynbos honey to taste

Personal Tasting Notes

Judges' Comments

Dense, spicy and bright with spicy oak and taut acidity. Savoury and fresh.

Wine Details

Wine of origin	Hemel-en-Aarde Valley
Alcohol level	13.23%
Residual Sugar g/L	2.33
Total Acid g/L	7.1
pH	3.16
Closure type	Cork
Single vineyard	n/a
Grape varietals	Chard
Percentage	100%
Irrigated	yes
Farm method	n/a
Debut vintage	1981
Total bottles produced	74 496
Approx retail price	R 290
Vinification	The wine spends 8 months in small French oak barrels. It stays on the lees for the full 8 months with battonage every 2nd week.
Oaking	French oak for 8 months.
Maturation	Barrel fermentation, barrel ageing 8 months. 34% 1st fill, 26% 2nd fill, 23% 3rd fill, 7% 4th fill. Wooding 100% 228L.
Ageing potential	8-10 years

Winemaker Notes

Tight and minerally, classic Hamilton Russell Vineyards length and complexity. Prominent pear and lime aromas. Flavours brought beautifully into focus by tight line of bright natural acid.

Producer Details

Vineyard/Producer	Hamilton Russell Vineyards
Physical address	R320, Hemel-en-Aarde Valley, Hermanus
Map page	278
GPS co-ordinates	S 34° 24' 16.3" E 019° 13' 15"
Established	1975
Owner	Anthony Hamilton Russell
Cellarmaster	n/a
Winemaker	Hannes Storm
Viticulturist	Johan Montgomery
First bottled vintage	1981
Area under vines	52 ha
Main varieties	Pinot, Chard
Red : white ratio	50 : 50
Total bottle production	138 384

Contact Details

Tel	028 312 3595
Email	talitahrv@hermanus.co.za
Web	www.hamiltonrussellvineyards.co.za
Tasting days & hours	Mon-Fri 9-5; Sat 9-1
Tasting fee	Complimentary; groups by appointment
Attractions	Estate olive oil & fynbos honey to taste

Personal Tasting Notes

Judges' Comments

Some roast coffee and eucalypt character with sweet black cherry and berry fruit.

HAMILTON RUSSELL VINEYARDS

Pinot noir

WALKER BAY WINE OF ORIGIN
MADE, MATURED AND BOTTLED ON HAMILTON RUSSELL VINEYARDS.
HEMEL-EN-AARDE VALLEY, HERMANUS, CAPE OF GOOD HOPE.

PRODUCE OF SOUTH AFRICA

Alc. 13.5% Vol.

Wine Details

Wine of origin	Hemel-en-Aarde Valley
Alcohol level	13.7%
Residual Sugar g/L	3.19
Total Acid g/L	6
pH	3.4
Closure type	Cork
Single vineyard	n/a
Grape varietals	Pinot
Percentage	100%
Irrigated	yes
Farm method	n/a
Debut vintage	1981
Total bottles produced	63 888
Approx retail price	R 290
Vinification	Barrel maturation 100%. 10 months barrel ageing. 100% MLF.
Oaking	French oak for 10 months.
Maturation	Barrel ageing 10 months. 44% 1st fill, 23% 2nd fill, 29% 3rd fill, 4% 4th fill. Wooding 100% 228L French oak barrels.
Ageing potential	8-10 years

Winemaker Notes

Low vigour, stony, clay-rich soil, cool maritime mesoclimate, naturally tiny yields of under 30 hl/ha and our philosophy of expressing terroir in our wines give rise to a certain tightness.

Producer Details

Vineyard/Producer	Jean Daneel Wines
Physical address	110 Sarel Ciller Street, Napier, Overberg
Map page	281
GPS co-ordinates	S 34° 27' 55.7" E 019° 53' 45.4"
Established	1997
Owner	Jean Daneel
Cellarmaster	Jean Daneel
Winemaker	Jean-Pierre Daneel
Viticulturist	Jean Daneel
First bottled vintage	1997
Area under vines	1.5 ha
Main varieties	Sauv B, Chen Bl, Shiraz, Merl
Red : white ratio	40 : 60
Total bottle production	45 000

Contact Details

Tel	028 423 3724
Email	adri@owcollection.co.za
Web	www.jdwines.co.za
Tasting days & hours	Tue-Sat 9-4
Tasting fee	R 20
Other attractions	Spectacular views

Personal Tasting Notes

Judges' Comments

Buttery, honeyed. Lively palate but with a soft oxidative finish.

Wine Details

Wine of origin	Western Cape
Alcohol level	14%
Residual Sugar g/L	3.5
Total Acid g/L	5.7
pH	3.34
Closure type	Cork
Single vineyard	n/a
Grape varietals	Chen Bl
Percentage	100%
Irrigated	no
Farm method	org
Debut vintage	2000
Total bottles produced	6 500
Approx retail price	R 96
Vinification	Not specified
Oaking	French oak for 12 months.
Maturation	12 months in French oak. 20% new oak is used.
Ageing potential	10 years

Winemaker Notes

Tones of lime, lemon skin, honeysuckle, baked apples, ripe pineapple and dried apricots which show in the acidity of the wine. Rich creamy palate with a complex fruity aftertaste.

Producer Details

Vineyard/Producer	Jordan Wine Estate
Physical address	Stellenbosch Kloof Road, Vlottenburg, Stellenbosch
Map page	268-269
GPS co-ordinates	S 33° 56' 33.7" E 018° 44' 41.3"
Established	1982
Owner	Jordan Family
Cellarmaster	Gary & Kathy Jordan
Winemaker	Sjaak Nelson
Viticulturist	Gary Jordan
First bottled vintage	1993
Area under vines	105 ha
Main varieties	Cab Sauv, Merl, Shiraz, Sauv B, Chard, Chen Bl
Red : white ratio	45 : 55
Total bottle production	50 000

Contact Details

Tel	021 881 3441
Email	juanita@jordanwines.com
Web	www.jordanwines.com
Tasting days & hours	Mon-Fri 9.30-4.30
Tasting fee	R 25
Other attractions	Cellar tours (by appointment), restaurant, fly fishing

Personal Tasting Notes

_____

_____

_____

_____

_____

_____

Judges' Comments

Pithy, taut, round and restrained with complex peach and toast notes as well as some quince character.

Wine Details

Wine of origin	Stellenbosch
Alcohol level	14.12%
Residual Sugar g/L	2.4
Total Acid g/L	6.3
pH	3.51
Closure type	Screw cap
Single vineyard	n/a
Grape varietals	Chard
Percentage	100%
Irrigated	yes
Farm method	n/a
Debut vintage	1997
Total bottles produced	34 197
Approx retail price	R 140
Vinification	Juice barrel fermented in 228L French oak barrels, 51% new, 49% 2nd fill. After maturation, 8% tank-fermented Chard was blended with the barrel-fermented wine.
Oaking	9 months in French oak. 51% new and 49% 2nd fill.
Maturation	Matured sur lie in the barrel for 9 months with occasional rolling of the barrels to accentuate the leesy character.
Ageing potential	Up to 5 years from vintage if stored correctly

Winemaker Notes

A powerful expression of Chardonnay, brimming with fruit and elegance. A buttery toastiness from the oak rounds off the complex hazelnut and citrus flavours.

Producer Details

Vineyard/Producer	Jordan Wine Estate
Physical address	Stellenbosch Kloof Road, Vlottenburg, Stellenbosch
Map page	268-269
GPS co-ordinates	S 33° 56′ 33.7″ E 018° 44′ 41.3″
Established	1982
Owner	Jordan Family
Cellarmaster	Gary & Kathy Jordan
Winemaker	Sjaak Nelson
Viticulturist	Gary Jordan
First bottled vintage	1993
Area under vines	105 ha
Main varieties	Cab Sauv, Merl, Shiraz, Sauv B, Chard, Chen Bl
Red : white ratio	45 : 55
Total bottle production	50 000

Contact Details

Tel	021 881 3441
Email	juanita@jordanwines.com
Web	www.jordanwines.com
Tasting days & hours	Mon-Fri 9.30-4.30
Tasting fee	R 25
Other attractions	Cellar tours (by appointment), restaurant, fly fishing

Personal Tasting Notes

Judges' Comments

Subtle vanilla pod as well as pear and apple fruit. Attractively spicy with some richness.

Wine Details

Wine of origin	Stellenbosch
Alcohol level	14.11%
Residual Sugar g/L	3.7
Total Acid g/L	6.9
pH	3.39
Closure type	Screw cap
Single vineyard	n/a
Grape varietals	Chen Bl
Percentage	100%
Irrigated	yes
Farm method	n/a
Debut vintage	1997
Total bottles produced	19 804
Approx retail price	R 97
Vinification	Juice barrel fermented in 228L 2nd fill French barrels, matured sur lie for 8 months. 32% tank-fermented Chen Bl was blended with the barrel-fermented portion.
Oaking	Lightly oaked for 8 months in French oak, 2nd fill.
Maturation	8 months sur lie with occasional barrel rolling.
Ageing potential	Up to 4 years if stored correctly

Winemaker Notes

A contemporary delicious mouth-filling experience of citrus cream, tropical fruit and honey interlaced with a spicy complexity.

Producer Details

Vineyard/Producer	Jordan Wine Estate
Physical address	Stellenbosch Kloof Road, Vlottenburg, Stellenbosch
Map page	268-269
GPS co-ordinates	S 33° 56′ 33.7″ E 018° 44′ 41.3″
Established	1982
Owner	Jordan Family
Cellarmaster	Gary & Kathy Jordan
Winemaker	Sjaak Nelson
Viticulturist	Gary Jordan
First bottled vintage	1993
Area under vines	105 ha
Main varieties	Cab Sauv, Merl, Shiraz, Sauv B, Chard, Chen Bl
Red : white ratio	45 : 55
Total bottle production	50 000

Contact Details

Tel	021 881 3441
Email	juanita@jordanwines.com
Web	www.jordanwines.com
Tasting days & hours	Mon-Fri 9.30-4.30
Tasting fee	R 25
Other attractions	Cellar tours (by appointment), restaurant, fly fishing

Personal Tasting Notes

Judges' Comments

Rich and opulent with some fruit sweetness but also some restraint – pear, spice and white peach notes.

The ultimate expression of the Jordan terroir. This limited release flagship wine is the culmination of the synergy between soil and soul.

JORDAN
STELLENBOSCH

Nine Yards 2010

ESTATE WINE *of* SOUTH AFRICA

Wine Details

Wine of origin	Stellenbosch
Alcohol level	14.44%
Residual Sugar g/L	3.3
Total Acid g/L	6.7
pH	3.27
Closure type	Screw cap
Single vineyard	Yes
Grape varietals	Chard
Percentage	100%
Irrigated	yes
Farm method	n/a
Debut vintage	2002
Total bottles produced	9 939
Approx retail price	R 290

Vinification	Juice barrel fermented in 228L French oak barrels. A percentage went through natural fementation. Matured for 12 months sur lie with regular barrel rolling.
Oaking	12 months in French oak. 92% new and 8% 2nd fill.
Maturation	The wine was matured sur lie for 12 months with regular barrel rolling.
Ageing potential	Up to 6 years from vintage if stored correctly

Winemaker Notes

Butterscotch, spicy cloves, lemon/lime, orange peel, complex mineral citrus flavours. Rich mouthfeel, subtly balanced by toasty French oak, integrates with long peach and melon finish.

Producer Details

Vineyard/Producer	Jordan Wine Estate
Physical address	Stellenbosch Kloof Road, Vlottenburg, Stellenbosch
Map page	268-269
GPS co-ordinates	S 33° 56' 33.7" E 018° 44' 41.3"
Established	1982
Owner	Jordan Family
Cellarmaster	Gary & Kathy Jordan
Winemaker	Sjaak Nelson
Viticulturist	Gary Jordan
First bottled vintage	1993
Area under vines	105 ha
Main varieties	Cab Sauv, Merl, Shiraz, Sauv B, Chard, Chen Bl
Red : white ratio	45 : 55
Total bottle production	50 000

Contact Details

Tel	021 881 3441
Email	juanita@jordanwines.com
Web	www.jordanwines.com
Tasting days & hours	Mon-Fri 9.30-4.30
Tasting fee	R 25
Other attractions	Cellar tours (by appointment), restaurant, fly fishing

Personal Tasting Notes

Judges' Comments

Honeyed vanilla/marzipan aromas. Complex. Palate has body, texture and depth. Serious, good acidity and freshness. Balanced. Toasty.

Wine Details

Wine of origin	Stellenbosch
Alcohol level	13.73%
Residual Sugar g/L	4.1
Total Acid g/L	6.2
pH	3.26
Closure type	Screw cap
Single vineyard	Yes
Grape varietals	Sauv B
Percentage	100%
Irrigated	yes
Farm method	n/a
Debut vintage	1993
Total bottles produced	6 984
Approx retail price	R 120

Vinification	Grapes 6-10 hours skin contact. Pressed, inoculated. Fermented in 60% new, 40% 2nd fill barrels. 8 months sur lie, occasional battonage. 40% tank-fermented Sauv B added.
Oaking	8 months in 90% French oak, 10% American oak.
Maturation	8 months sur lie with occasional battonage.
Ageing potential	5 years from vintage if stored correctly

Winemaker Notes

Ripe fig, gooseberry and tropical fruit flavours are complemented by the gently smoky vanilla nuances of oak.

Producer Details

Vineyard/Producer	Jordan Wine Estate
Physical address	Stellenbosch Kloof Road, Vlottenburg, Stellenbosch
Map page	268-269
GPS co-ordinates	S 33° 56′ 33.7″ E 018° 44′ 41.3″
Established	1982
Owner	Jordan Family
Cellarmaster	Gary & Kathy Jordan
Winemaker	Sjaak Nelson
Viticulturist	Gary Jordan
First bottled vintage	1993
Area under vines	105 ha
Main varieties	Cab Sauv, Merl, Shiraz, Sauv B, Chard, Chen Bl
Red : white ratio	45 : 55
Total bottle production	50 000

Contact Details

Tel	021 881 3441
Email	juanita@jordanwines.com
Web	www.jordanwines.com
Tasting days & hours	Mon-Fri 9.30-4.30
Tasting fee	R 25
Other attractions	Cellar tours (by appointment), restaurant, fly fishing

Personal Tasting Notes

Judges' Comments

Attractive floral notes. Citrus/lime flavour. Well balanced acidity, silky texture. Balanced sweetness.

2010 **THE REAL McCoy**
RIESLING ESTATE WINE OF SOUTH AFRICA

Wine Details

Wine of origin	Stellenbosch
Alcohol level	13.67%
Residual Sugar g/L	15
Total Acid g/L	7.2
pH	3.04
Closure type	Screw cap
Single vineyard	Yes
Grape varietals	Weisser Ries
Percentage	100%
Irrigated	yes
Farm method	n/a
Debut vintage	1993
Total bottles produced	6 222
Approx retail price	R 100

Vinification	Wine was tank fermented. Once a perfect balance between fruit and acidity was reached, the fermentation was stopped to retain a hint of natural residual sugar.
Oaking	Unoaked.
Maturation	n/a
Ageing potential	Up to 5 years if stored correctly

Winemaker Notes

Intense lemon/lime flavours. A crisp fruitiness makes it a superb partner with food. Hints of spiciness add to its intrigue.

Producer Details

Vineyard/Producer	Kanu Wines
Physical address	R304, Koelenhof, Stellenbosch
Map page	268-269
GPS co-ordinates	S 33° 88′ 94.8″ E 018° 81′ 90.6″
Established	1998
Owner	Ben Truter Trust
Cellarmaster	Johan Grimbeek
Winemaker	Johan Grimbeek
Viticulturist	Wynand Pienaar
First bottled vintage	1998
Area under vines	25 ha
Main varieties	Cab Fr, Cab Sauv, Sauv B, Chard, Malb, Pet V
Red : white ratio	50 : 50
Total bottle production	300 000

Contact Details

Tel	021 865 2488
Email	monique@kanu.co.za
Web	www.kanu.co.za
Tasting days & hours	Mon-Fri 9-4
Tasting fee	Complimentary
Other attractions	n/a

Personal Tasting Notes

Judges' Comments

Bold, rich and complex with ripe pear and melon fruit, good length with nice texture. A very bold style.

Wine Details

Wine of origin	Stellenbosch
Alcohol level	13%
Residual Sugar g/L	12.4
Total Acid g/L	6.6
pH	3.29
Closure type	Synthetic
Single vineyard	n/a
Grape varietals	Chen Bl
Percentage	100%
Irrigated	no
Farm method	n/a
Debut vintage	2011
Total bottles produced	4 416
Approx retail price	R 85
Vinification	Grapes destemmed, crushed, 6 hours skin contact, pressed. Left 48 hours to settle. Juice racked off lees and into barrels, 2.5% lees added. Fermentation.
Oaking	8 months in 46% French, 27% Hungarian and 27% American oak.
Maturation	8 months in barrels. Barrels rolled once every fortnight.
Ageing potential	5-7 years

Winemaker Notes

The oak is beautifully integrated with fruit and the wine has a lingering dry finish. A perfect wine with food as it evolves flavours whilst keeping its uniqueness.

Producer Details

Vineyard/Producer	Ken Forrester Wines
Physical address	Scholtzenhof Farm, corner R44 & Winery Road, Stellenbosch
Map page	274-275
GPS co-ordinates	S 34° 01′ 31 06″ E 018° 49′ 05 92″
Established	1993
Owner	Ken Forrester
Cellarmaster	Ken Forrester
Winemaker	Ken Forrester
Viticulturist	Pieter Rossouw
First bottled vintage	1994
Area under vines	25 ha
Main varieties	Chen Bl, Shiraz, Mourv, Gren
Red : white ratio	35 : 65
Total bottle production	840 000

Contact Details

Tel	021 855 2374
Email	admin@kenforresterwines.com
Web	www.kenforresterwines.com
Tasting days & hours	Mon-Fri 9-5; Sat 9.30-3.30
Tasting fee	R 30 (7 wines), R 50 (10 wines)
Other attractions	Dalewood cheese & charcuterie platters

Personal Tasting Notes

Judges' Comments

A rich, ripe, showy style with apricot and crystalline fruit. Nice red apple, pear and spice palate with some sweetness.

2010

THE
FMC

FORRESTER MEINERT CHENIN

CHENIN BLANC

KEN FORRESTER WINES SOUTH AFRICA

Wine Details

Wine of origin	Stellenbosch
Alcohol level	14.5%
Residual Sugar g/L	10.6
Total Acid g/L	6.5
pH	3.6
Closure type	Synthetic & cork
Single vineyard	n/a
Grape varietals	Chen Bl
Percentage	100%
Irrigated	yes
Farm method	n/a
Debut vintage	2000
Total bottles produced	18 900
Approx retail price	R 325

Vinification	NDVI photographic imagery is used to reveal identical growth, hence development and ripeness of individual vines. Grapes destemmed, crushed, no skin contact.
Oaking	French oak for 12 months.
Maturation	Natural yeast ferment (8-9 months) in new French oak. After 1 year selected barrels blended depending on structure and flavour.
Ageing potential	10 years

Winemaker Notes

This vintage is for keeping and should show well after 10 years. The pinnacle of what we consider to be the finest expression of the grapes of this varietal – an icon Chenin.

Producer Details

Vineyard/Producer	Klein Constantia
Physical address	Klein Constantia Road, Constantia
Map page	267
GPS co-ordinates	S 34° 2' 19.0" E 018° 24' 46.5"
Established	1986
Owner	Zdenek Bakala & Charles Harman
Cellarmaster	Matthew Day
Winemaker	Matthew Day
Viticulturist	Stiaan Cloete
First bottled vintage	1986
Area under vines	7 ha
Main varieties	Sauv B, Cab Sauv, Muscat de Frontignan
Red : white ratio	30 : 70
Total bottle production	360 000

Contact Details

Tel	021 794 5188
Email	jessica@kleinconstantia.com
Web	www.kleinconstantia.com
Tasting days & hours	Mon-Fri 9-5; Sat 9-3, Sun & Pub Hols closed
Tasting fee	Complimentary
Other attractions	n/a

Personal Tasting Notes

Judges' Comments

Inky black colour, very appealing blackcurrant nose along with mint chocolate, rasberry and violet perfume. A well-structured wine with fine-grained tannins and integrated cedar oak.

Wine Details

Wine of origin	Constantia
Alcohol level	14.6%
Residual Sugar g/L	2.9
Total Acid g/L	5.2
pH	3.75
Closure type	Cork
Single vineyard	n/a
Grape varietals	Cab Sauv
Percentage	100%
Irrigated	yes
Farm method	fair
Debut vintage	1986
Total bottles produced	19 500
Approx retail price	R 150

Vinification	Vinified at 28°C in upright open tanks. Fractions fermented into small wooden open-top tanks. 28°C extended skin contact after fermentation.
Oaking	French oak for 24 months.
Maturation	The wine spent a period of 24 months maturing in French oak barriques before bottling in Apr 2010.
Ageing potential	8 years

Winemaker Notes

Distinctly Cabernet Sauvignon aromas with touches of sandalwood and cassis.

Producer Details

Vineyard/Producer	Klein Constantia
Physical address	Klein Constantia Road, Constantia
Map page	267
GPS co-ordinates	S 34° 2' 19.0" E 018° 24' 46.5"
Established	1986
Owner	Zdenek Bakala & Charles Harman
Cellarmaster	Matthew Day
Winemaker	Matthew Day
Viticulturist	Stiaan Cloete
First bottled vintage	1986
Area under vines	7 ha
Main varieties	Sauv B, Cab Sauv, Muscat de Frontignan
Red : white ratio	30 : 70
Total bottle production	360 000

Contact Details

Tel	021 794 5188
Email	jessica@kleinconstantia.com
Web	www.kleinconstantia.com
Tasting days & hours	Mon-Fri 9-5; Sat 9-3, Sun & Pub Hols closed
Tasting fee	Complimentary
Other attractions	n/a

Personal Tasting Notes

Judges' Comments

Sweet and rich with some raisined character as well as orange and ripe melon fruit. Viscous, honeyed and sweet.

KLEIN CONSTANTIA
Estate Wine
Vin de Constance
2007
Natural Sweet Wine
Wine of South Africa

Wine Details

Wine of origin	Constantia
Alcohol level	14%
Residual Sugar g/L	177
Total Acid g/L	8.3
pH	3.5
Closure type	Cork & wax
Single vineyard	n/a
Grape varietals	Muscat de Frontignan
Percentage	100%
Irrigated	yes
Farm method	n/a
Debut vintage	1986
Total bottles produced	26 500
Approx retail price	R 300
Vinification	Grapes hand picked, left to macerate on skins for several days. Nectar obtained fermented in combination of stainless steel tanks and wooden 500L barrels.
Oaking	New 500L French and Hungarian 40% new oak barrels for 48 months.
Maturation	Total maturation time in cellar before bottling was 4 years.
Ageing potential	20 years

Winemaker Notes

Burnished copper colour, alluring aromas of Turkish Delight intermingle with fragrant honeysuckle, citrus peel and clove spiciness. Unctuously sweet, deeply complex. Long, vibrant finish.

Producer Details

Vineyard/Producer	La Motte
Physical address	R45 Main Street, Franschhoek
Map page	271
GPS co-ordinates	S 33° 53' 0.91" E 019° 4' 21.57"
Established	1969
Owner	Hanneli Rupert-Koegelenberg
Cellarmaster	Edmund Terblanche
Winemaker	Michael Langenhoven
Viticulturist	Pietie Le Roux
First bottled vintage	1985
Area under vines	75 ha
Main varieties	Sauv B, Chard, Shiraz, Merl, Pinot
Red : white ratio	50 : 50
Total bottle production	720 000

Contact Details

Tel	021 876 8000
Email	jjl.cellar@la-motte.co.za
Web	www.la-motte.com
Tasting days & hours	Mon-Sat 9-5
Tasting fee	R 30
Other attractions	Restaurant, farm shop, art museum, hiking trail

Personal Tasting Notes

Judges' Comments

Exciting black pepper and blackberry aromas. Savoury, refreshing notes of black olives give this refreshing red its immediacy.

Wine Details

Wine of origin	Western Cape	
Alcohol level	13.67%	
Residual Sugar g/L	2	
Total Acid g/L	5.9	
pH	3.54	
Closure type	Cork	
Single vineyard	n/a	
Grape varietals	Shiraz	Viog
Percentage	90%	10%
Irrigated	yes	yes
Farm method	n/a	n/a
Debut vintage	2003	
Total bottles produced	24 000	
Approx retail price	R 189	

Vinification	Shiraz and Viog hand sorted and placed in the tank together. Pumped over regularly and fermented at 25°C, after which wine was left on the lees for 2 weeks.
Oaking	French oak for 15 months.
Maturation	Malolactic fermentation and maturation were in 300L French oak barrels of which 70% new. Wine was matured for 15 months.
Ageing potential	6-10 years

Winemaker Notes

A wine full of flavour and complexity. The nose reflects black cherry and cranberry fruit with liquorice and white pepper spice. The splash of Viognier contributes with rose-petal perfume.

Special offer

FREE GIFT WRAPPING & DELIVERY

R149-00
inclusive of
gift wrapping
and postage

Gift a Top 100 SA Wine book to a friend today
Email info@top100sawines.com for bank details
R149 inclusive of book, gift wrapping & postage

THE GREENWOOD GUIDE TO
SOUTH AFRICA
hand-picked accommodation

- We spend 5 months each year visiting places to stay across the whole of South Africa.
- We include in the guide only those places that excel in character, friendliness and the hostly arts.
- All the descriptions are written by us, not the owners and each place is revisited each year.
- Published in book and web formats every spring.
- Eleventh edition published in May/June 2012.

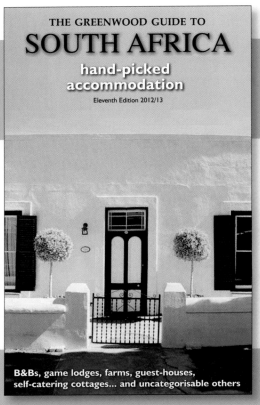

THE GREENWOOD GUIDE TO
SOUTH AFRICA
hand-picked accommodation
Eleventh Edition 2012/13

B&Bs, game lodges, farms, guest-houses, self-catering cottages... and uncategorisable others

www.greenwoodguides.com

Producer Details

Vineyard/Producer	La Motte
Physical address	R45 Main Street, Franschhoek
Map page	271
GPS co-ordinates	S 33° 53′ 0.91″ E 019° 4′ 21.57″
Established	1969
Owner	Hanneli Rupert-Koegelenberg
Cellarmaster	Edmund Terblanche
Winemaker	Michael Langenhoven
Viticulturist	Pietie Le Roux
First bottled vintage	1985
Area under vines	75 ha
Main varieties	Sauv B, Chard, Shiraz, Merl, Pinot
Red : white ratio	50 : 50
Total bottle production	720 000

Contact Details

Tel	021 876 8000
Email	jjl.cellar@la-motte.co.za
Web	www.la-motte.com
Tasting days & hours	Mon-Sat 9-5
Tasting fee	R 30
Other attractions	Restaurant, farm shop, art museum, hiking trail

Personal Tasting Notes

Judges' Comments

Taut, fine red fruits on the nose. Very fine with some matchstick, mineral notes. Fresh, vivid, youthful palate.

La Motte

2009
SHIRAZ

PRIVATE CELLAR, FRANSCHHOEK VALLEY
SOUTH AFRICA

Wine Details

Wine of origin	Western Cape			
Alcohol level	13.75%			
Residual Sugar g/L	2.5			
Total Acid g/L	5.7			
pH	3.55			
Closure type	Cork			
Single vineyard	n/a			
Grape varietals	Shiraz	Gren	Cins	Carig
Percentage	93.5%	3%	2.5%	1%
Irrigated	yes	no	no	no
Farm method	n/a	n/a	n/a	n/a
Debut vintage	1985			
Total bottles produced	198 000			
Approx retail price	R 125			

Vinification	Bunches destemmed, hand sorted. Whole berries pumped into open stainless steel tank, inoculated, cool fermented 20-24°C. During pump over, high aeration allowed.
Oaking	French oak for 14 months.
Maturation	MLF started in the tank and finished in 300L French oak barrels, 30% new. The wine was matured for 14 months.
Ageing potential	6-10 years

Winemaker Notes

Intense spicy nose with aniseed, clove, black pepper surrounded by black cherry, blueberry. Full-bodied palate, chewy and juicy, integrated wood tannin creates a pleasant clean, dry finish.

Producer Details

Vineyard/Producer	Landau du Val
Physical address	La Brie, Robertsvlei Road, Franschhoek
Map page	271
GPS co-ordinates	S 33° 55' 34.3" E 019° 6' 34.1"
Established	1905
Owner	Basil Landau
Cellarmaster	n/a
Winemaker	Anina Guelpa
Viticulturist	Martin du Plessis
First bottled vintage	1995
Area under vines	15 ha
Main varieties	Sem
Red : white ratio	100% white
Total bottle production	1 500

Contact Details

Tel	082 410 1130
Email	basillandau@mweb.co.za
Web	n/a
Tasting days & hours	n/a
Tasting fee	n/a
Other attractions	n/a

Personal Tasting Notes

Judges' Comments

Attractive ginger, clove, marzipan and candied orange peel flavours made this wine very appealing. Weighty yet with silky texture. Well-judged residual sugar.

Wine Details

Wine of origin	Franschhoek
Alcohol level	14%
Residual Sugar g/L	32
Total Acid g/L	5.3
pH	3.58
Closure type	Cork
Single vineyard	n/a
Grape varietals	Sem
Percentage	100%
Irrigated	no
Farm method	n/a
Debut vintage	1995
Total bottles produced	1 500
Approx retail price	R 190
Vinification	Grapes hand picked early morning, cooled down until next morning. Whole bunch pressed, settled overnight in cold conditions. Clear juice racked from fine lees.
Oaking	French oak.
Maturation	Cold conditions in tank for first 10°B, barrels for rest. 12 months 30% new French. Monthly battonage, light filter.
Ageing potential	Up to 10 years

Winemaker Notes

Gooseberry, apricot and other tropical notes such as papaya is prominent on the nose. Good oak/acid balance to fruit. Fresh acidity that changes to a full palate. Full-throttle but elegant.

Producer Details

Vineyard/Producer	L'Avenir
Physical address	R44, Klapmuts Road, Stellenbosch
Map page	268-269
GPS co-ordinates	S 33° 53′ 18.7″ E 018° 50′ 59.1″
Established	1992
Owner	Advini
Cellarmaster	Tinus Els
Winemaker	Tinus Els
Viticulturist	Tinus Els & Dirk Coetzee
First bottled vintage	1992
Area under vines	63 ha
Main varieties	Chen Bl, Sauv B, Chard, Ptage, Cab Sauv, Merl
Red : white ratio	51 : 49
Total bottle production	150 000

Contact Details

Tel	021 889 5001
Email	winesales@lavenir.co.za
Web	n/a
Tasting days & hours	Mon-Fri 8-5; Sat 10-4
Tasting fee	R 15 for 6 wines
Other attractions	Cellar tours (by appointment), lodge, BYO picnics

Personal Tasting Notes

_____

_____

_____

_____

_____

_____

Judges' Comments

Thick, dense, concentrated wine with blueberries, damson and plums, supported by prominent new oak which needs time to integrate.

Wine Details

Wine of origin	Stellenbosch
Alcohol level	14.04%
Residual Sugar g/L	2.4
Total Acid g/L	5.9
pH	3.61
Closure type	Cork
Single vineyard	Yes, Block 2
Grape varietals	Ptage
Percentage	100%
Irrigated	yes
Farm method	n/a
Debut vintage	2004
Total bottles produced	3 260
Approx retail price	R 250
Vinification	7 blocks of Pinotage are situated on various aspects of the large hill that comprises L'Avenir. Certain blocks were isolated for specific vinification styles.
Oaking	18 months in new French Never and Allier oak barrels.
Maturation	18 months in new French Never and Allier oak and 5 months in bottle.
Ageing potential	10 years +

Winemaker Notes

Ripe black cherries, plums, chocolate on nose. Rich plummy fruit and complex oak flavours that linger in the mouth ending with ample soft ripe tannins. Will mature well over the next decade.

Producer Details

Vineyard/Producer	Le Riche
Physical address	Leef op Hoop Farm, Jonkershoek Valley, Stellenbosch
Map page	268-269
GPS co-ordinates	S 33° 56' 26.5" E 018° 54' 14.3"
Established	1996
Owner	Etienne le Riche
Cellarmaster	Etienne le Riche
Winemaker	Christo le Riche
Viticulturist	n/a
First bottled vintage	1997
Area under vines	n/a
Main varieties	Cab Sauv
Red : white ratio	90 : 10
Total bottle production	60 000

Contact Details

Tel	021 887 0789
Email	wine@leriche.co.za
Web	www.leriche.co.za
Tasting days & hours	By appointment
Tasting fee	Complimentary
Other attractions	n/a

Personal Tasting Notes

Judges' Comments

A very juicy charismatic wine full of liquer cherries, After Eight mints, cassis. Soft and approachable style with silky tannins and long finish.

Wine Details

Wine of origin	Stellenbosch
Alcohol level	14.5%
Residual Sugar g/L	1.8
Total Acid g/L	6.4
pH	3.71
Closure type	Cork
Single vineyard	n/a
Grape varietals	Cab Sauv
Percentage	100%
Irrigated	yes
Farm method	n/a
Debut vintage	1997
Total bottles produced	6 000
Approx retail price	R 360

Vinification	Grapes hand selected. Fermentation with selected yeast, manual plunging. Closed tank maceration 10-14 days. Tanks, barrel for MLF. Aged in barrel and bottle.
Oaking	French oak for 22 months.
Maturation	22 months in 70% new 225L French oak barrels.
Ageing potential	7-10 years from vintage

Winemaker Notes

Dark fruit, cherry aromas with cedary oak and hints of spearmint on nose. Palate has full, smooth entry followed by structured mid-palate with balanced tannins. Elegant wine, long finish.

Producer Details

Vineyard/Producer	Nelson Wine Estate
Physical address	R44 Agter-Paarl, Windmeul
Map page	272-273
GPS co-ordinates	S 33° 39′ 31.2″ E 018° 56′ 17.3″
Established	1993
Owner	Alan Nelson
Cellarmaster	Lisha Nelson
Winemaker	Lisha Nelson
Viticulturist	Petrus de Villiers & Daniel Nelson
First bottled vintage	1993
Area under vines	46 ha
Main varieties	Shiraz, Cab Sauv, Merl, Cab Fr, Pet V, Sauv Bl
Red : white ratio	75 : 25
Total bottle production	120 000

Contact Details

Tel	021 869 8453
Email	lisha@nelsonscreek.co.za
Web	www.nelsonscreek.co.za
Tasting days & hours	By appointment
Tasting fee	Complimentary
Other attractions	Wedding & function venue

Personal Tasting Notes

Judges' Comments

Sweet, brooding, slightly meaty note. Blackberry fruit here is quite open and elegant with good structure.

Lisha Nelson

SIGNATURE RANGE

CABERNET FRANC

2008

Wine Details

Wine of origin	Paarl
Alcohol level	14.52%
Residual Sugar g/L	5.7
Total Acid g/L	5.7
pH	3.41
Closure type	Cork
Single vineyard	n/a
Grape varietals	Cab Fr
Percentage	100%
Irrigated	yes
Farm method	n/a
Debut vintage	2008
Total bottles produced	4 200
Approx retail price	R 200

Vinification	Strict crop reduction in vineyard. Hand picking and sorting. Cold soak and long spontanous alcoholic ferment on skins.
Oaking	French oak barrels for 22 months.
Maturation	22 months in 100% new French oak barrels followed by a couple of years bottle maturation.
Ageing potential	10 years

Winemaker Notes

This wine has a good colour and structure, lovely berry flavours on the nose with prominent blueberry and blackcurrant notes. Well rounded on the palate with lingering smooth aftertaste.

Producer Details

Vineyard/Producer	Lomond
Physical address	PO Box 184, Stellenbosch
Map page	281
GPS co-ordinates	S 34° 34' 12" E 019° 26' 24.00"
Established	1999
Owner	Distell & Lomond Properties
Cellarmaster	Kobus Gerber
Winemaker	Kobus Gerber
Viticulturist	Wayne Gabb
First bottled vintage	2005
Area under vines	800 ha
Main varieties	Merl, Syrah, Nouv, Sauv B
Red : white ratio	40 : 60
Total bottle production	Not specified

Contact Details

Tel	021 809 8330
Email	ekrige@capelegends.co.za
Web	www.lomond.co.za
Tasting days & hours	Closed to public, wine can be tasted at Farm 215
Tasting fee	n/a
Other attractions	n/a

Personal Tasting Notes

Judges' Comments

Lively grapefruit and mandarin. Lovely precision, broad but sure-footed. Refreshing lemon citrus. High level of intensity.

The Vineyards of
LOMOND
are situated in an area rich in
indigenous flora known as 'fynbos' at
CAPE AGULHAS.
The complexity
and distinctive character of the
PINCUSHION
VINEYARD
Sauvignon blanc
is an expression of the aspect,
soils and climate of
this single vineyard from the
2010 VINTAGE.
The vineyards are distinguished
by their cool coastal location at
the southern most tip of
SOUTH AFRICA.

Wine Details

Wine of origin	Cape Agulhas
Alcohol level	13.88%
Residual Sugar g/L	3.8
Total Acid g/L	6.9
pH	3.1
Closure type	Synthetic
Single vineyard	Yes
Grape varietals	Sauv B
Percentage	100%
Irrigated	yes
Farm method	bio
Debut vintage	Not specified
Total bottles produced	Not specified
Approx retail price	R 106
Vinification	Not specified
Oaking	Unoaked.
Maturation	n/a
Ageing potential	Not specified

Winemaker Notes

Brilliantly clear with green tinges. Whiffs of ripe fig, gooseberry, sweet tropical fruit, perfumed lavender. Ripe fig and tropical fruit follow through to the palate. A full-bodied wine.

Producer Details

Vineyard/Producer	Lomond
Physical address	PO Box 184, Stellenbosch
Map page	281
GPS co-ordinates	S 34° 34' 12" E 019° 26' 24.00"
Established	1999
Owner	Distell & Lomond Properties
Cellarmaster	Kobus Gerber
Winemaker	Kobus Gerber
Viticulturist	Wayne Gabb
First bottled vintage	2005
Area under vines	800 ha
Main varieties	Merl, Syrah, Nouv, Sauv B
Red : white ratio	40 : 60
Total bottle production	Not specified

Contact Details

Tel	021 809 8330
Email	ekrige@capelegends.co.za
Web	www.lomond.co.za
Tasting days & hours	Closed to public, wine can be tasted at Farm 215
Tasting fee	n/a
Other attractions	n/a

Personal Tasting Notes

Judges' Comments

Fragrant and attractive with blueberry fruit, a sumptuous ripe palate with rich meaty fruit.

The Vineyards of
LOMOND
are situated in an area rich in
indigenous flora known as "fynbos" at
CAPE AGULHAS.
The complexity
and distinctive character of the
CONEBUSH
VINEYARD
Syrah
is an expression of the aspect,
soils and climate of
this single vineyard from the
2008 VINTAGE.
The vineyards are distinguished
by their cool coastal location at
the southern most tip of
SOUTH AFRICA.

Wine Details

Wine of origin	Cape Agulhas
Alcohol level	14.91%
Residual Sugar g/L	2.3
Total Acid g/L	5.6
pH	3.61
Closure type	Synthetic
Single vineyard	Yes
Grape varietals	Shiraz
Percentage	100%
Irrigated	yes
Farm method	bio
Debut vintage	Not specified
Total bottles produced	Not specified
Approx retail price	R 236
Vinification	Hand picked and sorted, destemmed. Crushed into stainless steel, yeast inoculation. Fermentation. 3 weeks on skins. Pressed into 1st fill barrels. MLF, racked.
Oaking	18 months.
Maturation	18 months in the same barrels. Only the most excellent barrels were selected for fining, filtration prior to bottling.
Ageing potential	Not specified

Winemaker Notes

Dark ruby, aromas of black and red fruit with nuances of pepper spice and cloves while fresh violets contribute to complex bouquet. Beautiful, integrated, elegant wine with complex flavour.

Producer Details

Vineyard/Producer	Lomond
Physical address	PO Box 184, Stellenbosch
Map page	281
GPS co-ordinates	S 34° 34' 12" E 019° 26' 24.00"
Established	1999
Owner	Distell & Lomond Properties
Cellarmaster	Kobus Gerber
Winemaker	Kobus Gerber
Viticulturist	Wayne Gabb
First bottled vintage	2005
Area under vines	800 ha
Main varieties	Merl, Syrah, Nouv, Sauv B
Red : white ratio	40 : 60
Total bottle production	Not specified

Contact Details

Tel	021 809 8330
Email	ekrige@capelegends.co.za
Web	www.lomond.co.za
Tasting days & hours	Closed to public, wine can be tasted at Farm 215
Tasting fee	n/a
Other attractions	n/a

Personal Tasting Notes

Judges' Comments

Bright, exotic passion fruit, candied orange peel. This wine has power and richness combined with a fresh vibrant intensity. Very good.

Wine Details

Wine of origin	Cape Agulhas
Alcohol level	13.89%
Residual Sugar g/L	1.3
Total Acid g/L	6.8
pH	3.34
Closure type	Synthetic
Single vineyard	Yes
Grape varietals	Sauv B
Percentage	100%
Irrigated	yes
Farm method	bio
Debut vintage	Not specified
Total bottles produced	Not specified
Approx retail price	R 106
Vinification	Grapes harvested by hand at 22.5º-23º balling, handled reductively. Juice cold fermented at 13º-15°C. Left on the lees for 8 weeks before being racked.
Oaking	Unoaked.
Maturation	n/a
Ageing potential	Not specified

Winemaker Notes

Brilliantly clear colour with green tinges. Delicate aromas of citrus, pineapple and a mix of tropical fruits. Elegant palate with fresh acidity that balances out the intense fruit flavours.

Producer Details

Vineyard/Producer	Lomond
Physical address	PO Box 184, Stellenbosch
Map page	281
GPS co-ordinates	S 34° 34' 12" E 019° 26' 24.00"
Established	1999
Owner	Distell & Lomond Properties
Cellarmaster	Kobus Gerber
Winemaker	Kobus Gerber
Viticulturist	Wayne Gabb
First bottled vintage	2005
Area under vines	800 ha
Main varieties	Merl, Syrah, Nouv, Sauv B
Red : white ratio	40 : 60
Total bottle production	Not specified

Contact Details

Tel	021 809 8330
Email	ekrige@capelegends.co.za
Web	www.lomond.co.za
Tasting days & hours	Closed to public, wine can be tasted at Farm 215
Tasting fee	n/a
Other attractions	n/a

Personal Tasting Notes

Judges' Comments

Attractive lime and lemon citrus. On palate, delicate orange blossom and lemon thyme flavours over a forthright and clear, vibrant and deep palate. Savoury stuff.

The Vineyards of
LOMOND
are situated in an area rich in
indigenous flora known as "fynbos" at
CAPE AGULHAS.
The complexity
and distinctive character of the
SUGARBUSH
VINEYARD
Sauvignon blanc
is an expression of the unique
soils and climate of
this single vineyard from the
2010 VINTAGE.
The vineyards are distinguished
by their cool coastal location at
the southern most tip of
SOUTH AFRICA.

Wine Details

Wine of origin	Cape Agulhas
Alcohol level	13.95%
Residual Sugar g/L	4.3
Total Acid g/L	7
pH	3.14
Closure type	Synthetic
Single vineyard	Yes
Grape varietals	Sauv B
Percentage	100%
Irrigated	yes
Farm method	bio
Debut vintage	Not specified
Total bottles produced	Not specified
Approx retail price	R 106
Vinification	Grapes harvested by hand at 23º-24º balling, handled reductively. Juice cold fermented at 13º-15ºC. Left on the lees for 8 weeks before being racked.
Oaking	Unoaked.
Maturation	n/a
Ageing potential	Not specified

Winemaker Notes

Brilliantly clear colour with green tinges. Intense ripe figs, asparagus and granadilla aromas. Full bodied with an intense concentration of fruit flavours and lingering aftertaste.

Producer Details

Vineyard/Producer	Longridge
Physical address	Off R44, between Stellenbosch & Somerset West
Map page	274-275
GPS co-ordinates	S 34° 0' 55.2" E 018° 49' 60.0"
Established	2006
Owner	Aldo van der Laan
Cellarmaster	Jasper Raats
Winemaker	Jasper Raats
Viticulturist	Albert le Roux
First bottled vintage	2007
Area under vines	45 ha
Main varieties	Chard, Cab Sauv, Ptage, Chen Bl, Cab Fr, Shiraz
Red : white ratio	50 : 50
Total bottle production	290 000

Contact Details

Tel	021 855 2004
Email	info@top100sawines.co.za
Web	www.longridge.co.za
Tasting days & hours	Mon-Fri 9-5; Sat 9-2
Tasting fee	R 20 for 5 wines
Other attractions	Restaurant, open Fri-Tues

Personal Tasting Notes

Judges' Comments

The base wine appeared to have a good level of richness with toasted nuts, nougat and yellow apple which have developed well under bottle age.

Wine Details

Wine of origin	Western Cape	
Alcohol level	12.71%	
Residual Sugar g/L	6.4	
Total Acid g/L	6.8	
pH	3.39	
Closure type	Cork	
Single vineyard	n/a	
Grape varietals	Chard	Pinot
Percentage	82%	18%
Irrigated	yes	yes
Farm method	n/a	n/a
Debut vintage	2010	
Total bottles produced	260 000	
Approx retail price	R 108	

Vinification	Whole bunch pressed, settled. 3°C for 2 nights. Chard racked, ferment in oak. Pinot racked, ferment in steel. MLF. On gross lees 5 months. 2nd ferment in bottle.
Oaking	Unoaked.
Maturation	22 months lees contact in the bottle before being disgorged and labeled, ready for drinking.
Ageing potential	Ready for drinking

Winemaker Notes

Lingering, vibrant mousse brings to the surface flavours and aromas of lime leaf, roasted almond, hints of caramelised green apple, citrus, ripe strawberry. Ends with fine, fresh minerality.

Producer Details

Vineyard/Producer	Longridge
Physical address	Off R44, between Stellenbosch & Somerset West
Map page	274-275
GPS co-ordinates	S 34° 0' 55.2" E 018° 49' 60.0"
Established	2006
Owner	Aldo van der Laan
Cellarmaster	Jasper Raats
Winemaker	Jasper Raats
Viticulturist	Albert le Roux
First bottled vintage	2007
Area under vines	45 ha
Main varieties	Chard, Cab Sauv, Ptage, Chen Bl, Cab Fr, Shiraz
Red : white ratio	50 : 50
Total bottle production	290 000

Contact Details

Tel	021 855 2004
Email	info@top100sawines.co.za
Web	www.longridge.co.za
Tasting days & hours	Mon-Fri 9-5; Sat 9-2
Tasting fee	R 20 for 5 wines
Other attractions	Restaurant, open Fri-Tues

Personal Tasting Notes

Judges' Comments

Savoury, slightly rubbery edge to the fruit here. Taut, pithy and focussed with pear and quince character.

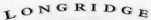

LONGRIDGE

2009
CHARDONNAY

WINE OF SOUTH AFRICA

Wine Details

Wine of origin	Western Cape
Alcohol level	13.54%
Residual Sugar g/L	2.2
Total Acid g/L	6.4
pH	3.46
Closure type	Cork
Single vineyard	n/a
Grape varietals	Chard
Percentage	100%
Irrigated	yes
Farm method	n/a
Debut vintage	2010
Total bottles produced	39 424
Approx retail price	R 89

Vinification	Harvested in morning cool, 2 hours skin contact, whole bunch pressed. Juice naturally settled and racked to 70% new 225L and 300L French oak for natural fermentation.
Oaking	5 months in French oak.
Maturation	Left on its gross lees for 6 months before racking. Wine then put back into barrel for further 5 months.
Ageing potential	3-5 years

Winemaker Notes

Light straw colour, vibrant scents of lime, grapefruit, honeycomb and almond brittle. Natural fermentation in French oak gave a full mid-palate, exotic flavours and a pleasant crisp finish.

Producer Details

Vineyard/Producer	Longridge
Physical address	Off R44, between Stellenbosch & Somerset West
Map page	274-275
GPS co-ordinates	S 34° 0' 55.2" E 018° 49' 60.0"
Established	2006
Owner	Aldo van der Laan
Cellarmaster	Jasper Raats
Winemaker	Jasper Raats
Viticulturist	Albert le Roux
First bottled vintage	2007
Area under vines	45 ha
Main varieties	Chard, Cab Sauv, Ptage, Chen Bl, Cab Fr, Shiraz
Red : white ratio	50 : 50
Total bottle production	290 000

Contact Details

Tel	021 855 2004
Email	info@top100sawines.co.za
Web	www.longridge.co.za
Tasting days & hours	Mon-Fri 9-5; Sat 9-2
Tasting fee	R 20 for 5 wines
Other attractions	Restaurant, open Fri-Tues

Personal Tasting Notes

Judges' Comments

Attractive berry fruits and cassis. Tight and refined with polished tannic structure.

LONGRIDGE

2008
MERLOT

STELLENBOSCH • SOUTH AFRICA

BEST
VALUE
AWARD
SA WINES

Wine Details

Wine of origin	Stellenbosch
Alcohol level	14%
Residual Sugar g/L	3
Total Acid g/L	5.7
pH	3.53
Closure type	Cork
Single vineyard	n/a
Grape varietals	Merl
Percentage	100%
Irrigated	yes
Farm method	n/a
Debut vintage	2010
Total bottles produced	44 470
Approx retail price	R 107

Vinification	Meticulous sorting. Cold soaked 28 hours (under inert gas). Part natural fermentation, part inoculated. 8 days fermentation, left on skins for a week. Pressed.
Oaking	French oak for 15 months.
Maturation	The wine spent 15 months in a combination of new (57%) and older French barrels.
Ageing potential	5 years

Winemaker Notes

Out of the deep garnet colour comes the aroma of deep plum, red cherry and dark chocolate aromas. The palate is balanced with silky tannins and undertones of cured ham.

Producer Details

Vineyard/Producer	Louis Wines
Physical address	3 Chestnut Lane, Stellenbosch
Map page	268-269
GPS co-ordinates	S 33° 55′ 06.29″ E 018° 50′ 58.37″
Established	2007
Owner	Louis Nel
Cellarmaster	Louis Nel
Winemaker	Louis Nel
Viticulturist	Louis Nel
First bottled vintage	2007
Area under vines	n/a
Main varieties	Cab Sauv, Sauv B
Red : white ratio	50 : 50
Total bottle production	18 000

Contact Details

Tel	021 889 5555
Email	louis@louiswines.com
Web	www.louiswines.com
Tasting days & hours	By appointment
Tasting fee	Complimentary
Other attractions	n/a

Personal Tasting Notes

Judges' Comments

Deeply coloured, persistent menthol, blackcurrant aromas. Ripe fruit with dense structured savoury tannins. Developing well. A ripe, complex wine. Well handled.

Wine Details

Wine of origin	Stellenbosch
Alcohol level	14.78%
Residual Sugar g/L	1.4
Total Acid g/L	6
pH	3.76
Closure type	Cork
Single vineyard	n/a
Grape varietals	Cab Sauv
Percentage	100%
Irrigated	no
Farm method	n/a
Debut vintage	2007
Total bottles produced	2 700
Approx retail price	R 240
Vinification	Natural fermentation. One week on the skins. 24 months French oak barrels, 30% new.
Oaking	French oak for 24 months.
Maturation	As per oaking regime.
Ageing potential	20 years

Winemaker Notes

Wild berries, ripe plum, cassis and luscious cedar flavours abound on the nose. Red berries, plum follow through onto palate and complement soft chewy tannins that create a lingering finish.

Producer Details

Vineyard/Producer	Miles Mossop Wines
Physical address	Helshoogte Pass, Stellenbosch
Map page	268-269
GPS co-ordinates	S 33° 55′ 06.12″ E 018° 55′ 16.87″
Established	2001
Owner	Miles Mossop
Cellarmaster	Miles Mossop
Winemaker	Miles Mossop
Viticulturist	Aidan Morton
First bottled vintage	2004
Area under vines	n/a
Main varieties	Cab Sauv, Chen Bl, Merl, Pet V, Viog
Red : white ratio	40 : 60
Total bottle production	8 000

Contact Details

Tel	082 413 4335
Email	miles@milesmossopwines.com
Web	www.milesmossopwines.com
Tasting days & hours	By appointment
Tasting fee	Complimentary
Other attractions	Deli, restaurant, oliveshed

Personal Tasting Notes

Judges' Comments

*Smooth, rich, ripe black fruits with a hint of tea leaf and herbs.
Plummy and generous with nice texture.*

2008

Max

MILES MOSSOP WINES   SOUTH AFRICA

Wine Details

Wine of origin	Coastal		
Alcohol level	14.44%		
Residual Sugar g/L	31.4		
Total Acid g/L	0.59		
pH	3.71		
Closure type	Screw Cap		
Single vineyard	n/a		
Grape varietals	Cab Sauv	Pet V	Merl
Percentage	50%	27%	23%
Irrigated	n/a	n/a	n/a
Farm method	n/a	n/a	n/a
Debut vintage	2010		
Total bottles produced	5 928		
Approx retail price	R 151		

Vinification	Grapes ripened to peak maturity. Hand harvested, cold store 4°C. Small open wooden fermenters, natural fermentation by yeast up to 14 days. Regular punch downs.
Oaking	French oak for 10 months.
Maturation	MLF in barrel. Racked, returned for further maturation. 38% new French barriques. Light egg-white fining, no filtration.
Ageing potential	5-8 years

Winemaker Notes

Stunning deep garnet colour. Heady nose of ripe fresh prunes, dark cherries, cocoa, cassis. Palate full and rich with savoury notes. Dark cherry, Christmas cake and dark chocolate flavours.

Producer Details

Vineyard/Producer	Super Single Vineyards
Physical address	Canettevallei Wine and Lavender Farm, Stellenbosch Kloof Road
Map page	268-269
GPS co-ordinates	S 33° 56' 29. 73" E 018° 45' 15. 20"
Established	2007
Owner	Daniel De Waal
Cellarmaster	Daniel De Waal
Winemaker	Daniel De Waal & Kyle Zulch
Viticulturist	Daniel De Waal & Kyle Zulch
First bottled vintage	2007
Area under vines	60 ha
Main varieties	Sutherland: Syrah
Red : white ratio	60 : 40
Total bottle production	10 300

Contact Details

Tel	021 881 3026
Email	marketing@ssvineyards.co.za
Web	www.supersinglevineyards.co.za
Tasting days & hours	Tasting Room under construction: opening Oct '12
Tasting fee	n/a
Other attractions	n/a

Personal Tasting Notes

Judges' Comments

Ripe, sweet meaty nose with olive and garrigue notes. Lush and fresh with lovely complexity. Intriguing.

Mount SUTHERLAND

2009 SYRAH

SUTHERLAND-KAROO
South Africa

Wine Details

Wine of origin	Sutherland, Karoo
Alcohol level	14.5%
Residual Sugar g/L	1.8
Total Acid g/L	5.6
pH	3.55
Closure type	Cork
Single vineyard	Yes, Kanolfontein Vineyard
Grape varietals	Syrah
Percentage	100%
Irrigated	yes
Farm method	org
Debut vintage	2009
Total bottles produced	4 800
Approx retail price	R 190

Vinification	Cold soaked for 10 days. Low temperature fermentation. Pumped over 3 times daily. Fermented dry. Free-run and press juice used. Post maceration.
Oaking	French oak for 15 months.
Maturation	15 months in French oak barrels, 20% new.
Ageing potential	8 years +

Winemaker Notes

Continental-style Syrah. Aromas of rose petals, black cherries, cloves, freshly milled white pepper. Tremendous succulence and richness on the palate ending in a pleasant, long, ripe finish.

Producer Details

Vineyard/Producer	Mulderbosch
Physical address	Goedgeloof Farm, Polkadraai Road (M12), Stellenbosch
Map page	268-269
GPS co-ordinates	S 33° 56′ 56.1″ E 018° 45′ 57.2″
Established	1989
Owner	Terroir Capital
Cellarmaster	Adam Mason
Winemaker	Adam Mason
Viticulturist	Lucinda Heyns
First bottled vintage	1991
Area under vines	45.2 ha
Main varieties	Chen Bl, Nouv, Viog, Pet V, Shiraz, Cab Sauv
Red : white ratio	30 : 70
Total bottle production	150 x 12

Contact Details

Tel	021 881 8140
Email	naomi@mulderbosch.co.za
Web	www.mulderbosch.co.za
Tasting days & hours	Mon-Sat 10-6
Tasting fee	R 35 for the whole range
Other attractions	Authentic Italian wood-burning oven, Bocce lawn games

Personal Tasting Notes

Judges' Comments

Bold style with ripe peachy fruit. Some vanilla, coconut, pineapple fruit. Some pistachio. Zesty and intense, exotic and complex.

MULDERBOSCH

Wine Details

Wine of origin	Stellenbosch
Alcohol level	12.5%
Residual Sugar g/L	6.2
Total Acid g/L	7.1
pH	3.47
Closure type	Cork
Single vineyard	Yes, Koelenhof
Grape varietals	Chard
Percentage	100%
Irrigated	yes
Farm method	n/a
Debut vintage	1998
Total bottles produced	12 050
Approx retail price	R 199

Vinification	Grapes hand picked, 3 hours skin contact, pressed. Juice settled overnight, racked to French barriques with 3% of lees. Spontaneous fermentation after 4 days.
Oaking	French oak for 9 months.
Maturation	No MLF, left on the gross lees 9 months, barrels rolled 4 x a month. After maturation, lightly fined, filtered, bottled.
Ageing potential	6-9 years

Winemaker Notes

Green, gold hues. Entices the senses with vanilla, English country garden herbs, rolled oats, peach pip, chestnut and tangerine. Robust, round, sensual palate, lingers on the aftertaste.

Producer Details

Vineyard/Producer	Mulderbosch
Physical address	Goedgeloof Farm, Polkadraai Road (M12), Stellenbosch
Map page	268-269
GPS co-ordinates	S 33° 56' 56.1" E 018° 45' 57.2"
Established	1989
Owner	Terroir Capital
Cellarmaster	Adam Mason
Winemaker	Adam Mason
Viticulturist	Lucinda Heyns
First bottled vintage	1991
Area under vines	45.2 ha
Main varieties	Chen Bl, Nouv, Viog, Pet V, Shiraz, Cab Sauv
Red : white ratio	30 : 70
Total bottle production	150 x 12

Contact Details

Tel	021 881 8140
Email	naomi@mulderbosch.co.za
Web	www.mulderbosch.co.za
Tasting days & hours	Mon-Sat 10-6
Tasting fee	R 35 for the whole range
Other attractions	Authentic Italian wood-burning oven, Bocce lawn games

Personal Tasting Notes

Judges' Comments

Nutty and bold with green apple and pear fruit as well as grapefruit freshness. Pithy, slightly bitter finish and nice fruitiness.

MULDERBOSCH

Wine Details

Wine of origin	Western Cape	
Alcohol level	13.5%	
Residual Sugar g/L	6.5	
Total Acid g/L	6.9	
pH	3.26	
Closure type	Synthetic	
Single vineyard	n/a	
Grape varietals	Chen Bl	Viog
Percentage	95%	5%
Irrigated	yes	yes
Farm method	n/a	n/a
Debut vintage	1998	
Total bottles produced	132 085	
Approx retail price	R 59	

Vinification	Harvested early morning, crushed, lightly pressed. Must cold settled before inoculation with select yeast culture.
Oaking	Lightly oaked 5 months in new Hungarian and American, new and used French oak.
Maturation	81% tank fermented, 19% natural fermentation in barrel. Matured for 5 months in oak. Fined, sterile filtered, bottled.
Ageing potential	5-8 years

Winemaker Notes

Pale straw colour. Intense nose with Bartlett pear, red apple, tarragon, persimmon, lime peel. Broad and appealing mid-palate, surprising creamy texture, subtle jasmine and frangipane notes.

Producer Details

Vineyard/Producer	Mvemve Raats
Physical address	Vlaeberg Road, Polkadraai, Stellenbosch
Map page	268-269
GPS co-ordinates	S 33° 58′ 16.6″ E 018° 44′ 55.3″
Established	2004
Owner	Bruwer Raats + Mzokhona Mvemve
Cellarmaster	Bruwer Raats + Mzokhona Mvemve
Winemaker	Bruwer Raats + Mzokhona Mvemve
Viticulturist	Bruwer Raats + Mzokhona Mvemve
First bottled vintage	2004
Area under vines	n/a
Main varieties	Cab Fr, Cab Sauv, Malb, Pet V
Red : white ratio	100% red
Total bottle production	1 800

Contact Details

Tel	021 881 3078
Email	braats@mweb.co.za
Web	www.raats.co.za
Tasting days & hours	By appointment
Tasting fee	R 200 per group (1-10 people)
Other attractions	n/a

Personal Tasting Notes

Judges' Comments

Hint of mint with smooth, clean, ripe, pure berry fruits. Nicely stitched with lovely purity and good ageing potential.

Wine Details

Wine of origin	Stellenbosch				
Alcohol level	14.5%				
Residual Sugar g/L	1.5				
Total Acid g/L	6.1				
pH	3.59				
Closure type	Cork				
Single vineyard	n/a				
Grape varietals	Cab Fr	Cab Sauv	Malb	Pet V	Merl
Percentage	25%	25%	25%	12.5%	12.5%
Irrigated	yes	yes	yes	yes	yes
Farm method	n/a	n/a	n/a	n/a	n/a
Debut vintage	2004				
Total bottles produced	2 400				
Approx retail price	R 650				

Vinification	Components vinified separately. Tasted blind after 1 year in barrel. Blend constructed in descending percentages from wine rated highest to that in 5th place.
Oaking	French oak for 24 months.
Maturation	Each variety spent 12 months in barrel as a single varietal. After blending, the wine was matured for another 12 months.
Ageing potential	5-10 years

Winemaker Notes

Deep, dark intense ruby colour. Red plum and black cherry fruit with a hint of cinnamon. Rich and muscular with mineral, blackberry fruit and dark chocolate on the finish.

Producer Details

Vineyard/Producer	Neethlingshof
Physical address	R310, Polkadraai Road, Stellenbosch
Map page	268-269
GPS co-ordinates	S 35° 56' 28.2" E 018° 48' 6.7"
Established	1692
Owner	Distell & Lusan partnership
Cellarmaster	De Wet Viljoen
Winemaker	De Wet Viljoen
Viticulturist	Hannes van Zyl
First bottled vintage	1880
Area under vines	120 ha
Main varieties	Cab Sauv, Cab Fr, Malb, Merl, Pet V, Ptage
Red : white ratio	55 : 45
Total bottle production	300 000

Contact Details

Tel	021 883 8988
Email	lgradwell@capelegends.co.za
Web	www.neethlingshof.co.za
Tasting days & hours	Mon-Fri 9-5 (Dec-Jan 9-7); Sat & Sun 10-4 (Dec-Jan 10-6)
Tasting fee	R 30
Other attractions	Food & wine pairing (R 95 pp, booking required)

Personal Tasting Notes

Judges' Comments

Inky black, modern textbook Pinotage. Crunchy, blackcurrant freshness, good concentration with the density to pair with substantial cuisine.

Wine Details

Wine of origin	Stellenbosch
Alcohol level	14.37%
Residual Sugar g/L	1.2
Total Acid g/L	6.3
pH	3.72
Closure type	Cork
Single vineyard	n/a
Grape varietals	Ptage
Percentage	100%
Irrigated	no
Farm method	bio
Debut vintage	2007
Total bottles produced	3 600
Approx retail price	R 139

Vinification	Grapes harvested mid-Feb at 25° balling, yielding around 6 tons/ha. After destalking and crushing, mash was fermented using a selected pure yeast culture NT50.
Oaking	French and American oak for 14 months.
Maturation	Fermentation in rotation tanks at 25-28°C over 7 days, skins pressed. After MLF, matured in French and American oak.
Ageing potential	Enjoy now or mature for 10 years

Winemaker Notes

Dark red colour. Bouquet of ripe fruit and banana aromas with a background of vanilla oak. A rich and velvety palate with ripe fruit and vanilla flavour.

Producer Details

Vineyard/Producer	Nitida Cellars
Physical address	Maasspruit Farm, Old Tygerberg Valley Road, Durbanville
Map page	270
GPS co-ordinates	S 33° 50' 3.8" E 018° 35' 37"
Established	1995
Owner	Bernhard Veller
Cellarmaster	Bernhard Veller
Winemaker	RJ Botha
Viticulturist	RJ Botha
First bottled vintage	1995
Area under vines	16 ha
Main varieties	Sauv B, Sem, Ries, Cab Sauv, Merl, Cab Fr
Red : white ratio	70 : 30
Total bottle production	100 000

Contact Details

Tel	021 976 1467
Email	jacus@nitida.co.za
Web	www.nitida.co.za
Tasting days & hours	Mon-Fri 9.30-5; Sat 9.30-3; Sun & Pub Hols 11-3
Tasting fee	R 20 (refunded upon purchase)
Other attractions	2 restaurants, farmers' market, concerts

Personal Tasting Notes

Judges' Comments

Pure fresh notes with delicate notes of green sage, melon, apple, gooseberry and pear. Tightly structured and restrained. Well balanced.

CLUB SELECT SAUVIGNON BLANC

2011

WINE OF ORIGIN DURBANVILLE

Wine Details

Wine of origin	Durbanville
Alcohol level	12.93%
Residual Sugar g/L	2.6
Total Acid g/L	7
pH	3.32
Closure type	Synthetic
Single vineyard	n/a
Grape varietals	Sauv B
Percentage	100%
Irrigated	no
Farm method	n/a
Debut vintage	2001
Total bottles produced	3 300
Approx retail price	R 115

Vinification	Hand picked in two time slots at different degrees of ripeness. 24 hours skin contact – reductive winemaking practices followed by the blending of 2 tanks.
Oaking	Unoaked.
Maturation	Made totally reductive, 18-24 hour skin contact, 1 month lees contact.
Ageing potential	1-5 years

Winemaker Notes

Wide spectrum of flavours. The year allowed us to make our favourite more pyrazine-style Sauv B which holds well with good acids.

Producer Details

Vineyard/Producer	Oldenburg Vineyards
Physical address	Zevenrivieren Road, Helshoogte Pass, Banghoek, Stellenbosch
Map page	268-269
GPS co-ordinates	S 33° 55' 7.61" E 018° 56' 8.75"
Established	1960
Owner	Adrian Vanderspuy
Cellarmaster	n/a
Winemaker	Simon Thompson
Viticulturist	Simon Thompson
First bottled vintage	2008
Area under vines	30 ha
Main varieties	Cab Sauv, Cab Fr, Syrah, Merl, Chen Bl, Chard
Red : white ratio	65 : 35
Total bottle production	31 784

Contact Details

Tel	021 885 1618
Email	ina@oldenburgvineyards.com
Web	www.oldenburgvineyards.com
Tasting days & hours	Mon-Fri 10-4.30; Sat & Pub Hols by appointment
Tasting fee	R 25 for 5 wines
Other attractions	n/a

Personal Tasting Notes

Judges' Comments

Spicy black fruits on the nose with a palate showing complex fruit, some chalkiness and appropriate green notes. Elegant, varietally true.

Wine Details

Wine of origin	Banghoek, Stellenbosch
Alcohol level	14.5%
Residual Sugar g/L	17
Total Acid g/L	5.9
pH	3.7
Closure type	Cork
Single vineyard	n/a
Grape varietals	Cab Fr
Percentage	100%
Irrigated	yes
Farm method	n/a
Debut vintage	2008
Total bottles produced	5 600
Approx retail price	R 182

Vinification	Crushed and destemmed, 3 days cold soak in closed-top stainless steel tanks. Pump over 3-6 times per day. Natural fermentation.
Oaking	French oak for 16 months.
Maturation	Fermented dry, then racked to barrel to complete MLF. The wine was matured in 30% new French oak barrels.
Ageing potential	8-10 years

Winemaker Notes

Combination of lemon thyme and wild herb scents sprinkled with spice on the nose. On the palate, peach underscored by smooth tannins and juiciness. A spicy aftertaste lingers in the mouth.

Producer Details

Vineyard/Producer	Oldenburg Vineyards
Physical address	Zevenrivieren Road, Helshoogte Pass, Banghoek, Stellenbosch
Map page	268-269
GPS co-ordinates	S 33° 55' 7.61" E 018° 56' 8.75"
Established	1960
Owner	Adrian Vanderspuy
Cellarmaster	n/a
Winemaker	Simon Thompson
Viticulturist	Simon Thompson
First bottled vintage	2008
Area under vines	30 ha
Main varieties	Cab Sauv, Cab Fr, Syrah, Merl, Chen Bl, Chard
Red : white ratio	65 : 35
Total bottle production	31 784

Contact Details

Tel	021 885 1618
Email	ina@oldenburgvineyards.com
Web	www.oldenburgvineyards.com
Tasting days & hours	Mon-Fri 10-4.30; Sat & Pub Hols by appointment
Tasting fee	R 25 for 5 wines
Other attractions	n/a

Personal Tasting Notes

Judges' Comments

Fruity and round with apple, kiwi fruit, nuts, pear and peach, backed up by minty spicy oak.

Wine Details

Wine of origin	Banghoek, Stellenbosch	
Alcohol level	13%	
Residual Sugar g/L	3	
Total Acid g/L	6.2	
pH	3.35	
Closure type	Screw cap	
Single vineyard	n/a	
Grape varietals	Chen Bl	Chard
Percentage	86%	14%
Irrigated	yes	yes
Farm method	n/a	n/a
Debut vintage	2010	
Total bottles produced	3 984	
Approx retail price	R 118	

Vinification	Crushed and destemmed, pressed, fermentation takes place in barrel. Left on lees for 1 month, then racked, followed by regular lees stirring (battonage).
Oaking	French oak for 9 months.
Maturation	Matured in 50% new oak barrels for 9 months. The final blend is made up from both tank and barrel-fermented Chen Bl.
Ageing potential	5 years

Winemaker Notes

Beautiful layers of fruit and vanilla oak spice transforms into silky smooth finish. The zesty acidiy of the Chen Bl completes the balance with freshness and crisp rejuvenating minerality.

Producer Details

Vineyard/Producer	Overgaauw Wine Estate
Physical address	Stellenbosch Kloof Road, Vlottenburg
Map page	268-269
GPS co-ordinates	S 33° 56' 55.0" E 018° 47' 34.0"
Established	1905
Owner	Braam van Velden
Cellarmaster	David van Velden
Winemaker	David van Velden
Viticulturist	Vinpro
First bottled vintage	1970
Area under vines	35 ha
Main varieties	Sylv, Chard, Sauv B, Chen Bl, Ptage
Red : white ratio	60 : 40
Total bottle production	120 000

Contact Details

Tel	021 881 3815
Email	info@overgaauw.co.za
Web	www.overgaauw.co.za
Tasting days & hours	Mon-Fri 8.30-5; Sat 10-2
Tasting fee	Complimentary; groups of more than 6 - R 10 pp
Other attractions	Picnic area

Personal Tasting Notes

Judges' Comments

Smooth, gravelly, chalky edge to the ripe fruits on the nose. Open, lush palate with generous ripe black fruits. Attractive, grainy structure – traditional but well done.

Wine Details

Wine of origin	Stellenbosch		
Alcohol level	14%		
Residual Sugar g/L	1.6		
Total Acid g/L	5.9		
pH	3.68		
Closure type	Cork		
Single vineyard	n/a		
Grape varietals	Cab Sauv	Merl	Cab Fr
Percentage	57%	29%	14%
Irrigated	yes	yes	yes
Farm method	n/a	n/a	n/a
Debut vintage	1979		
Total bottles produced	1 990		
Approx retail price	R 159		

Vinification	Varietals fermented separately for average of 9 days on the skins at 26°C, maceration on skins for 10 days.
Oaking	French oak for 18 months
Maturation	Matured in 225L French oak barrels for 18 months. 60% new barrels, 40% 2nd fill barrels.
Ageing potential	At least 10 years

Winemaker Notes

Perfumed nose generously offers layers of cassis, raspberry, cedar and touch of spice and minerals. Nose follows through to well-balanced palate which delivers ripe tannins, brilliant fruit.

Producer Details

Vineyard/Producer	Paul Cluver Wines
Physical address	De Rust Estate, N2 (Kromco turn-off), Grabouw
Map page	278
GPS co-ordinates	S 34° 10′ 6.2″ E 019° 5′ 8.1″
Established	1997
Owner	Cluver Family
Cellarmaster	Andries Burger
Winemaker	Andries Burger
Viticulturist	Craig Harris
First bottled vintage	1997
Area under vines	82 ha
Main varieties	Pinot, Chard, Ries, Gewürz
Red : white ratio	30 : 70
Total bottle production	240 000

Contact Details

Tel	021 844 0605
Email	info@cluver.com
Web	www.cluver.com
Tasting days & hours	Mon-Fri 9-5; Sat 10-2
Tasting fee	Complimentary; groups of more than 6 - R 30 pp
Other attractions	Forest amphitheatre, restaurant, distillery

Personal Tasting Notes

Judges' Comments

Linear, focussed and precise with some spicy oak alongside the finely wrought fruit.

2010
CHARDONNAY

Wine Details

Wine of origin	Elgin
Alcohol level	13.83%
Residual Sugar g/L	2.8
Total Acid g/L	7
pH	3.45
Closure type	Synthetic
Single vineyard	n/a
Grape varietals	Chard
Percentage	100%
Irrigated	no
Farm method	n/a
Debut vintage	1997
Total bottles produced	36 000
Approx retail price	R 120
Vinification	100% barrel fermented. No yeast added for alcoholic fermentation. No inoculation for malolactic fermentation.
Oaking	French oak for 9 months
Maturation	Barrel rolling for lees contact. No stirring of lees.
Ageing potential	5-8 years

Winemaker Notes

No overt wood on nose. Subtle citrus fruit and citrus blossom fragrances with hints of vanilla pod and almond flakes. Fine, fresh acidity is natural, adding poise and focus to the wine.

Producer Details

Vineyard/Producer	Rickety Bridge Winery
Physical address	R45 Main Road, Franschhoek
Map page	271
GPS co-ordinates	S 33° 53' 58.5" E 019° 5' 27.6"
Established	2000
Owner	DS Sarnia (Pty) Ltd
Cellarmaster	Wynand Grobler
Winemaker	Wynand Grobler & Danie de Bruyn
Viticulturist	Wynand Grobler
First bottled vintage	1993
Area under vines	26 ha
Main varieties	Cab Sauv, Sauv B, Chen Bl, Sem, Chard, Shiraz
Red : white ratio	55 : 45
Total bottle production	120 000

Contact Details

Tel	021 876 2129
Email	info@ricketybridge.com
Web	www.ricketybridge.com
Tasting days & hours	Mon-Sun 10-5
Tasting fee	R 20 for 5 wines
	(refunded upon purchase)
Other attractions	Restaurant, guest house, boules

Personal Tasting Notes

Judges' Comments

Intensely floral South African take on Côte Rôtie that is very drinkable now with its fresh rasberry flavours and perfectly judged oak flavours.

Wine Details

Wine of origin	Western Cape				
Alcohol level	14.22%				
Residual Sugar g/L	3.3				
Total Acid g/L	5.8				
pH	3.61				
Closure type	Cork				
Single vineyard	n/a				
Grape varietals	Syrah	Mourv	Gren	Cins	Tann
Percentage	54%	12%	9%	12%	13%
Irrigated	yes	yes	yes	no	no
Farm method	n/a	n/a	n/a	org	org
Debut vintage	2008				
Total bottles produced	16 300				
Approx retail price	R 85				

Vinification	Natural whole bunch ferment with 3-5 punch downs daily.
Oaking	French oak for 18 months.
Maturation	Old 500L barrels for 18 months.
Ageing potential	5 years

Winemaker Notes

Juicy raspberry, mulberry aromas, hints of chocolate. Layers of complex spice and red berry fruit fill the entire mouth. Well-integrated, seamless tannins emphasise spice on lengthy finish.

Producer Details

Vineyard/Producer	Rietvallei Wine Estate
Physical address	R60 between Robertson & Ashton, Robertson
Map page	280
GPS co-ordinates	S 33° 49′ 36″ E 019° 58′ 39″
Established	1864
Owner	Johnny Burger
Cellarmaster	Kobus Burger
Winemaker	Kobus Burger
Viticulturist	Kobus Burger
First bottled vintage	1975
Area under vines	180 ha
Main varieties	Sauv B, Chard, Chen Bl, Cab Sauv, Shiraz
Red : white ratio	30 : 70
Total bottle production	500 000

Contact Details

Tel	023 626 3596
Email	lezaan@rietvallei.co.za
Web	www.rietvallei.co.za
Tasting days & hours	Mon-Fri 8-5; Sat & Pub Hols 10-2
Tasting fee	Complimentary; R 10 pp for a group
Other attractions	n/a

Personal Tasting Notes

Judges' Comments

Interesting lemon curd, apple notes in a flinty restrained style. Bright acidity, elegant wine, slight hollow on mid-palate which will come forward with bottle age.

Wine Details

Wine of origin	Robertson			
Alcohol level	12.93%			
Residual Sugar g/L	2.2			
Total Acid g/L	7.5			
pH	3.28			
Closure type	Cork			
Single vineyard	Yes			
Grape varietals	Sauv B	Chard	Chen Bl	Viog
Percentage	56%	31%	12%	1%
Irrigated	n/a	n/a	n/a	n/a
Farm method	n/a	n/a	n/a	n/a
Debut vintage	2011			
Total bottles produced	2 400			
Approx retail price	R 120			

Vinification	Sauv B, Chen Bl partly tank fermented, transferred to new French oak halfway through fermentation. Chard barrel fermented in new French oak. Viog tank fermented
Oaking	French oak for 10 months.
Maturation	20% unoaked, tank cold-fermented Sauv B added to final blend. 10 months maturation on lees in the barrels and tanks.
Ageing potential	10 years +

Winemaker Notes

Green fig, melon aromas which follow through onto palate. Crisp acidity yet has a satisfying creamy weight. Lingering aftertaste hints at the pedigree and longevity of this delicious wine.

Producer Details

Vineyard/Producer	Rustenberg Wines
Physical address	Off Rustenburg Road, Idas Valley, Stellenbosch
Map page	268-269
GPS co-ordinates	S 33° 53′ 44.8″ E 018° 53′ 33.6″
Established	1682
Owner	Simon Barlow
Cellarmaster	Randolph Christians
Winemaker	Randolph Christians
Viticulturist	Nico Walters
First bottled vintage	1892
Area under vines	154 ha
Main varieties	Cab Sauv, Chard, Merl, Gren, Malb, Mourv, Rouss
Red : white ratio	56 : 44
Total bottle production	840 000

Contact Details

Tel	021 809 1200
Email	bernette@rustenberg.co.za
Web	www.rustenberg.co.za
Tasting days & hours	Mon-Fri 9-4.30; Sat 10-4; Sun 10-3
Tasting fee	R 25
Other attractions	Gardens

Personal Tasting Notes

Judges' Comments

Round and sweet with lush cassis and plum fruit. Bold and muscular with cherry grip on the palate. Sturdy and satisfying.

RUSTENBERG
Stellenbosch
John X Merriman
2009
SIMONSBERG-STELLENBOSCH
SOUTH AFRICA

Wine Details

Wine of origin	Simonsberg, Stellenbosch				
Alcohol level	14.61%				
Residual Sugar g/L	3.1				
Total Acid g/L	6.2				
pH	3.59				
Closure type	Cork				
Single vineyard	n/a				
Grape varietals	Cab Sauv	Merl	Pet V	Cab Fr	Malb
Percentage	51%	35%	7%	4%	3%
Irrigated	yes	yes	yes	yes	yes
Farm method	bio	bio	bio	bio	bio
Debut vintage	2011				
Total bottles produced	46 086				
Approx retail price	R 165				

Vinification	Rack and returns during primary fermentation at approximately 26°C in order to ensure maximum extraction followed by 3 weeks extended maceration on skins.
Oaking	21 months in 225L French oak. 46% new, 54% 2nd and 3rd fill.
Maturation	Wine was drained and gravity filled to barrels for malolactic fermentation.
Ageing potential	10-15 years from vintage

Winemaker Notes

Plum and cigar box aromas prelude a multi-layered palate with elegant tannin structure. This Bordeaux blend typifies Rustenberg terroir and has good ageing potential if cellared correctly.

Producer Details

Vineyard/Producer	Saronsberg Cellar
Physical address	Waveren Road, Tulbagh
Map page	277
GPS co-ordinates	S 33° 14' 48.2" E 019° 7' 2.0"
Established	2002
Owner	Saronsberg (Pty) Ltd
Cellarmaster	Dewaldt Heyns
Winemaker	Dewaldt Heyns
Viticulturist	Dewaldt Heyns
First bottled vintage	2004
Area under vines	45 ha
Main varieties	Shiraz
Red : white ratio	70 : 30
Total bottle production	180 000

Contact Details

Tel	023 230 0707
Email	leana@saronsberg.com
Web	www.saronsberg.com
Tasting days & hours	Mon-Fri 8.30-5; Sat 10-2
Tasting fee	R 25
Other attractions	Art gallery

Personal Tasting Notes

Judges' Comments

A hint of eucalyptus with well-judged sweet blackberry and plum fruit. Lovely bright fruit here.

Wine Details

Wine of origin	Coastal				
Alcohol level	14.5%				
Residual Sugar g/L	1.4				
Total Acid g/L	6.2				
pH	3.62				
Closure type	Cork				
Single vineyard	n/a				
Grape varietals	Cab Sauv	Merl	Malb	Pet V	Cab Fr
Percentage	53%	23%	11%	9%	4%
Irrigated	yes	yes	yes	yes	yes
Farm method	n/a	n/a	n/a	n/a	n/a
Debut vintage	2005				
Total bottles produced	45 600				
Approx retail price	R 110				

Vinification	Grapes force-cooled to 4°C, bunch sorted, destemmed, berry sorted and gently crushed into a satellite tank, then deposited into open and closed fermenters.
Oaking	French Allier oak barrels for 20 months.
Maturation	The wines were pressed into 36% new and 64% 2nd fill 300L French Allier barrels. The press fraction was separated.
Ageing potential	10 years

Winemaker Notes

The Provenance Rooi has a dark colour with flavours of cassis, red berry and integrated oak. The tannin is firm and well balanced with a full-bodied elegant finish.

Producer Details

Vineyard/Producer	Saronsberg Cellar
Physical address	Waveren Road, Tulbagh
Map page	277
GPS co-ordinates	S 33° 14' 48.2" E 019° 7' 2.0"
Established	2002
Owner	Saronsberg (Pty) Ltd
Cellarmaster	Dewaldt Heyns
Winemaker	Dewaldt Heyns
Viticulturist	Dewaldt Heyns
First bottled vintage	2004
Area under vines	45 ha
Main varieties	Shiraz
Red : white ratio	70 : 30
Total bottle production	180 000

Contact Details

Tel	023 230 0707
Email	leana@saronsberg.com
Web	www.saronsberg.com
Tasting days & hours	Mon-Fri 8.30-5; Sat 10-2
Tasting fee	R 25
Other attractions	Art gallery

Personal Tasting Notes

Judges' Comments

Ripe, spicy, vivid with lovely definition to the sweet blackberry and plum fruit. Taut, mineral undercurrents.

Wine Details

Wine of origin	Coastal
Alcohol level	14.5%
Residual Sugar g/L	2.4
Total Acid g/L	5.9
pH	3.58
Closure type	Cork
Single vineyard	n/a
Grape varietals	Shiraz
Percentage	100%
Irrigated	yes
Farm method	n/a
Debut vintage	2005
Total bottles produced	32 500
Approx retail price	R 110

Vinification	Grapes were hand picked in the early morning and force cooled to 4°C. Bunches sorted, destemmed and berries sorted on vibration tables.
Oaking	French Allier oak barrels for 18 months.
Maturation	8% new and 62% 2nd fill 300L Allier French oak barrels for a total of 18 months.
Ageing potential	11 years

Winemaker Notes

Deep, dark colour with soft ripe plum, red berry and floral flavours. The oak is well balanced with elegant and accessible tannins complemented by a touch of spice and full body.

Producer Details

Vineyard/Producer	Saronsberg Cellar
Physical address	Waveren Road, Tulbagh
Map page	277
GPS co-ordinates	S 33° 14′ 48.2″ E 019° 7′ 2.0″
Established	2002
Owner	Saronsberg (Pty) Ltd
Cellarmaster	Dewaldt Heyns
Winemaker	Dewaldt Heyns
Viticulturist	Dewaldt Heyns
First bottled vintage	2004
Area under vines	45 ha
Main varieties	Shiraz
Red : white ratio	70 : 30
Total bottle production	180 000

Contact Details

Tel	023 230 0707
Email	leana@saronsberg.com
Web	www.saronsberg.com
Tasting days & hours	Mon-Fri 8.30-5; Sat 10-2
Tasting fee	R 25
Other attractions	Art gallery

Personal Tasting Notes

Judges' Comments

Rich, lush and meaty with brooding ripe black fruits and crushed rock minerality. Stylish and defined.

SHIRAZ
2010

South Africa

Wine Details

Wine of origin	Tulbagh
Alcohol level	14.5%
Residual Sugar g/L	2.8
Total Acid g/L	6.2
pH	3.71
Closure type	Cork
Single vineyard	n/a
Grape varietals	Shiraz
Percentage	100%
Irrigated	yes
Farm method	n/a
Debut vintage	2004
Total bottles produced	20 000
Approx retail price	R 200

Vinification	The fermenting cap was manually punched down twice daily and 1 pump over per day. The rest was given extended maceration after fermentation.
Oaking	French Allier oak barrels for 20 months.
Maturation	The wine was pressed into 90% new and 10% 2nd fill Allier French oak barrels. Bottle maturation for 12 months.
Ageing potential	10 years

Winemaker Notes

The Shiraz has a deep, dark purple colour with prominent ripe plum, red berry and floral flavours with undertones of spice. The oak is well balanced with full, firm yet accessible tannins.

Producer Details

Vineyard/Producer	Saronsberg Cellar
Physical address	Waveren Road, Tulbagh
Map page	277
GPS co-ordinates	S 33° 14′ 48.2″ E 019° 7′ 2.0″
Established	2002
Owner	Saronsberg (Pty) Ltd
Cellarmaster	Dewaldt Heyns
Winemaker	Dewaldt Heyns
Viticulturist	Dewaldt Heyns
First bottled vintage	2004
Area under vines	45 ha
Main varieties	Shiraz
Red : white ratio	70 : 30
Total bottle production	180 000

Contact Details

Tel	023 230 0707
Email	leana@saronsberg.com
Web	www.saronsberg.com
Tasting days & hours	Mon-Fri 8.30-5; Sat 10-2
Tasting fee	R 25
Other attractions	Art gallery

Personal Tasting Notes

Judges' Comments

Pears, baked apple, dried apricots, peaches, very juicy and appealing. Succulent texture. Savoury and concentrated. Good varietal characters.

SARONSBERG

VIOGNIER
2010

South Africa

Wine Details

Wine of origin	Tulbagh
Alcohol level	13.5%
Residual Sugar g/L	3.7
Total Acid g/L	5.5
pH	3.41
Closure type	Cork
Single vineyard	n/a
Grape varietals	Viog
Percentage	100%
Irrigated	yes
Farm method	n/a
Debut vintage	2005
Total bottles produced	6 000
Approx retail price	R 110

Vinification	Only the first light pressings were used which were then oxidised to soften the phenolics on the end wine. The juice was settled at 5°C for 48 hours.
Oaking	French Allier oak barrels for 14 months.
Maturation	Total barrel maturation of 14 months, racked, protein stabilised and bottled. Further 12 months bottle maturation.
Ageing potential	6 years

Winemaker Notes

A light straw colour and flavours of butterscotch, nutty caramel, pear and lime. It has a rich, silky palate and a balanced oak finish. Complements foods with spicy aromas and flavours.

Producer Details

Vineyard/Producer	Saxenburg Wine Estate
Physical address	Polkedraai Road, between Stellenbosch / Kuilsriver
Map page	268-269
GPS co-ordinates	S 33° 56′ 47.9″ E 018° 43′ 9.4″
Established	1693
Owner	The Bührer Family
Cellarmaster	Nico van der Merwe
Winemaker	Nico van der Merwe & Edwin Grace (assistant)
Viticulturist	Donovan Diedericks
First bottled vintage	1710
Area under vines	90 ha
Main varieties	Sauv B, Shiraz
Red : white ratio	80 : 20
Total bottle production	300 000

Contact Details

Tel	021 903 6113
Email	info@saxenburg.co.za
Web	www.saxenburg.co.za
Tasting days & hours	Mon-Fri 9-5;
	Sat & Sun 10-4.30
Tasting fee	R 15 (4 wines),
	R 20 (6 wines)
Other attractions	Guest cottages, restaurant

Personal Tasting Notes

Judges' Comments

Olive, mint and violet nose with lovely sweet fruit. Bold and rich with lush blackberry fruit.

SAXENBURG
ANNO 1693

PRIVATE COLLECTION
SHIRAZ
2007
STELLENBOSCH

Wine Details

Wine of origin	Stellenbosch
Alcohol level	14%
Residual Sugar g/L	3.6
Total Acid g/L	5.8
pH	3.6
Closure type	Cork
Single vineyard	n/a
Grape varietals	Shiraz
Percentage	100%
Irrigated	yes
Farm method	n/a
Debut vintage	1990
Total bottles produced	36 000
Approx retail price	R 145

Vinification	Open tank fermentation at 30°C with plunging, pumping over 4 x daily. Skin contact for 3 weeks with MLF in tanks, no fining or filtration before barrel maturation.
Oaking	12 months in 80% American, 20% French oak.
Maturation	300L American (80%) and French (20%) oak. 30% new. Bottled Jan 2009.
Ageing potential	10 years +

Winemaker Notes

Elegant wine, ideal to mature for those special winter occasions. Warm spicy flavours and hints of coffee strikes a fine balance between fruit and tannins, but more red fruit flavours.

Producer Details

Vineyard/Producer	Shannon Vineyards
Physical address	Rockview Dam Road, Elgin
Map page	278
GPS co-ordinates	S 34° 11′ 3.9″ E 018° 59′ 3.6″
Established	2000
Owner	James & Stuart Downes
Cellarmaster	Gordon Newton Johnson
Winemaker	Nadia Newton Johnson
Viticulturist	James Downes & Kevin Watt
First bottled vintage	2007
Area under vines	15.5 ha
Main varieties	Sauv B, Sem, Viog, Pinot, Merl
Red : white ratio	50 : 50
Total bottle production	21 000

Contact Details

Tel	021 859 2491
Email	james@shannonwines.com
Web	www.shannonwines.com
Tasting days & hours	By appointment
Tasting fee	Complimentary
Other attractions	View over wetlands on the Palmiet River

Personal Tasting Notes

Judges' Comments

Lemon sherbet and lavender. Intense and charismatic, rich and concentrated. A rich, full, generously proportioned white.

SHANNON *vineyards*

Sanctuary Peak
SAUVIGNON BLANC 2011
ELGIN VALLEY • SOUTH AFRICA

Wine Details

Wine of origin	Elgin	
Alcohol level	13.5%	
Residual Sugar g/L	4.4	
Total Acid g/L	6.1	
pH	3.27	
Closure type	Synthetic	
Single vineyard	n/a	
Grape varietals	Sauv B	Sem
Percentage	88%	12%
Irrigated	yes	yes
Farm method	n/a	n/a
Debut vintage	2008	
Total bottles produced	5 620	
Approx retail price	R 108	

Vinification	Grapes chilled to 3°C. Sorted, destemmed, crushed. Selection undergoes skin contact at 8°C. Gentle press, juice settled 72 hours at 2°C. Fermentation in steel.
Oaking	Lightly oaked in 1st fill French oak for 3 months.
Maturation	12% blended Sem fermented on natural yeasts, matured 3 months in 100% new French oak. Battonnage practised fortnightly.
Ageing potential	15 years

Winemaker Notes

Very distinctive and concentrated primary fruit aromas of asparagus, citrus and some capsicum in a minerally, flinty style. Flavours on riper side of the fruit spectrum.

Producer Details

Vineyard/Producer	Simonsig Estate
Physical address	Kromme Rhee Road, Koelenhof
Map page	268-269
GPS co-ordinates	S 33° 52' 12.1" E 018° 49' 31.7"
Established	1953
Owner	Pieter, Francois & Johan Malan
Cellarmaster	Johan Malan
Winemaker	Johan Malan, Debbie Thompson & Hannes Meyer
Viticulturist	Francois Malan & Tommie Corbett
First bottled vintage	1968
Area under vines	210 ha
Main varieties	Ptage, Cab Sauv, Shiraz, Chard, Sauv B, Pinot
Red : white ratio	33% red, 47% white, 2% rosé, 18% MCC
Total bottle production	2.1 million

Contact Details

Tel	021 888 4900
Email	desireedev@simonsig.co.za
Web	www.simonsig.co.za
Tasting days & hours	Mon-Fri 8.30-5; Sat 8.30-4; Sun 11-3
Tasting fee	R 25 (glass included)
Other attractions	4x4 trail, vineyard walking trail, restaurant

Personal Tasting Notes

Judges' Comments

Strong, autolytic characters (mushroom, spicy, creamy brioche) with plenty of fruit. Well balanced with some residual sugar.

Wine Details

Wine of origin	Stellenbosch		
Alcohol level	12.45%		
Residual Sugar g/L	7.1		
Total Acid g/L	7.6		
pH	3.2		
Closure type	Cork		
Single vineyard	n/a		
Grape varietals	Pinot	Chard	Pinot Meunier
Percentage	58%	39%	3%
Irrigated	yes	yes	yes
Farm method	bio	bio	bio
Debut vintage	1971		
Total bottles produced	344 413		
Approx retail price	R 97		

Vinification	Grapes hand picked, whole bunch pressed in gentle action pneumatic presses. Juice fractioned and 1st pressing. 1-2 days settling, fermented 15-16°C. Some Chard goes through MLF.
Oaking	Lightly oaked, a portion of the Chardonnay is fermented in French oak.
Maturation	n/a
Ageing potential	4-6 years

Winemaker Notes

Lively, energetic mousse forming crown of bubbles. Rich, biscuity colour. Red berry aromas mix with sweet baked apple, sourdough yeasty complexity. Zesty citrus, freshly baked bread on palate.

Producer Details

Vineyard/Producer	Stark-Condé
Physical address	Jonkershoek Valley Road, Jonkershoek Valley, Stellenbosch
Map page	268-269
GPS co-ordinates	S 33° 57' 14.00" E 018° 54' 38.00"
Established	1998
Owner	José Conde
Cellarmaster	José Conde
Winemaker	José Conde
Viticulturist	Andrew Klink
First bottled vintage	1998
Area under vines	40 ha
Main varieties	Cab Sauv, Syrah, Cab Fr, Merl, Pet V
Red : white ratio	85 : 15
Total bottle production	45 000

Contact Details

Tel	021 861 7700
Email	info@stark-conde.co.za
Web	www.stark-conde.co.za
Tasting days & hours	Mon-Sun 10-4
Tasting fee	R 30 (5 wines), R 40 (all)
Other attractions	Tasting room on lake, Postcard Café

Personal Tasting Notes

Judges' Comments

Full-bodied, concentrated rasberry, blackcurrants, raisin fruit with a lovely freshness. Ripe and clear with spicy extended finish. Well knit.

Stark-Condé

Three Pines
Cabernet Sauvignon
unfined and unfiltered
2009
JONKERSHOEK VALLEY

Wine Details

Wine of origin	Jonkershoek Valley		
Alcohol level	14.52%		
Residual Sugar g/L	2.3		
Total Acid g/L	6		
pH	3.75		
Closure type	Cork		
Single vineyard	n/a		
Grape varietals	Cab Sauv	Pet V	Merl
Percentage	87.4%	7.6%	5%
Irrigated	yes	yes	yes
Farm method	n/a	n/a	n/a
Debut vintage	2000		
Total bottles produced	4 300		
Approx retail price	R 275		

Vinification	Grapes cooled to 14°C, crushed. Cold soaked, inoculated yeast. Hand punched down every 2-4 hours, every 6-8 hours till dry. Pressed, racked to barrel for MLF.
Oaking	22 months in 300L French oak.
Maturation	French oak (70% new) 18 months. Assembled, back to barrels for 4 months. Bottle unfined and unfiltered after barrel maturation.
Ageing potential	15 years

Winemaker Notes

Classic Cabernet aromas with violet notes, rich and intense on palate with silky smooth tannins.

Producer Details

Vineyard/Producer	Sumaridge Estate Wines
Physical address	Farm Cell 2 No.15, Upper Hemel-en-Aarde Valley, R320 (Caledon) Road, Hermanus
Map page	278
GPS co-ordinates	S 34° 22' 1.6" E 019° 15' 18.6"
Established	1997
Owner	Simon Turner & Holly Bellingham
Cellarmaster	Gavin Patterson
Winemaker	Gavin Patterson
Viticulturist	Gavin Patterson
First bottled vintage	2000
Area under vines	42 h
Main varieties	Chard, Pinot, Sauv B, Merl, Ptage, Shiraz
Red : white ratio	50 : 50
Total bottle production	150 000

Contact Details

Tel	028 312 1097
Email	gavin@sumaridge.co.za
Web	www.sumaridge.co.za
Tasting days & hours	Mon-Sun 10-3
Tasting fee	Complimentary; groups of more than 6 - R 10 pp (refunded upon purchase)
Other attractions	Accom, mountain biking, walking routes, wildlife

Personal Tasting Notes

Judges' Comments

Toasty, spicy, pithy with some gunsmoke and fruit notes and a structured palate. Taut and stylish.

SUMARIDGE

Chardonnay

CHARDONNAY 2010
UPPER HEMEL-EN-AARDE VALLEY
WALKER BAY | SOUTH AFRICA

Wine Details

Wine of origin	Upper Hemel-en-Aarde Valley
Alcohol level	13.67%
Residual Sugar g/L	2.2
Total Acid g/L	6.7
pH	3.23
Closure type	Cork
Single vineyard	n/a
Grape varietals	Chard
Percentage	100%
Irrigated	yes
Farm method	n/a
Debut vintage	2001
Total bottles produced	5 600
Approx retail price	R 140
Vinification	Destemmed, crushed, cooled through press, settled 36 hours. Racked to barrel for fermentation with selected yeast for 2 weeks.
Oaking	9 months in French oak. 228L tight grain MT (30% new).
Maturation	MLF inoculated onto firm lees with battonage until onset of MLF in autumn through winter. Assemblage late December.
Ageing potential	5 years +

Winemaker Notes

Typically lively minerality combines with lime, quince, citrus blossom as fresh flavours which augment the rich mouthfeel that lingers long on the aftertaste. Versatile wine of classic style.

Producer Details

Vineyard/Producer	Swartland Winery
Physical address	Farm "Doornkuil", R45, Malmesbury
Map page	276
GPS co-ordinates	S 33° 27' 12.7" E 018° 45' 17.7"
Established	1948
Owner	Shareholders
Cellarmaster	Andries Blake
Winemaker	Andries Blake
Viticulturist	Claud Uren
First bottled vintage	1948
Area under vines	2689 ha
Main varieties	Sauv B, Chen Bl, Shiraz, Merl, Cab Sauv, Ptage
Red : white ratio	60 : 40
Total bottle production	4 003 651

Contact Details

Tel	022 482 1134
Email	info@swwines.co.za
Web	www.swwines.co.za
Tasting days & hours	Mon-Fri 8-5; Sat 9-2
Tasting fee	Complimentary
Other attractions	n/a

Personal Tasting Notes

Judges' Comments

A deep, dense wine with plenty of ripe blackberry and blueberry fruit supported with a generous helping of oak that needs time to evolve.

Wine Details

Wine of origin	Swartland
Alcohol level	14.57%
Residual Sugar g/L	3.1
Total Acid g/L	5.66
pH	3.43
Closure type	Cork
Single vineyard	n/a
Grape varietals	Ptage
Percentage	100%
Irrigated	no
Farm method	n/a
Debut vintage	2011
Total bottles produced	8 244
Approx retail price	R 98
Vinification	Harvested at optimum ripeness. Gently crushed. Ferment in stainless steel. Pressed, inoculated for MLF. After MLF, racked, sterile filtrated, moved to barrels.
Oaking	French oak for 13 months.
Maturation	Racked after 4 months, aged 8 months more (temperature and humidity control). Tasted, selectively blended. Bottle aged few months.
Ageing potential	Drink now or store for 2-4 years

Winemaker Notes

Dark red, brick-red hue on glass. Intense plum and cherries on nose, dark spice, smokiness at the back. Fresh dark fruits on palate, firm but elegant tannins, lingering dark spice aftertase.

Producer Details

Vineyard/Producer	Swartland Winery
Physical address	Farm "Doornkuil", R45, Malmesbury
Map page	276
GPS co-ordinates	S 33° 27' 12.7" E 018° 45' 17.7"
Established	1948
Owner	Shareholders
Cellarmaster	Andries Blake
Winemaker	Andries Blake
Viticulturist	Claud Uren
First bottled vintage	1948
Area under vines	2689 ha
Main varieties	Sauv B, Chen Bl, Shiraz, Merl, Cab Sauv, Ptage
Red : white ratio	60 : 40
Total bottle production	4 003 651

Contact Details

Tel	022 482 1134
Email	info@swwines.co.za
Web	www.swwines.co.za
Tasting days & hours	Mon-Fri 8-5; Sat 9-2;
Tasting fee	Complimentary
Other attractions	n/a

Personal Tasting Notes

Judges' Comments

Vivid and precise with cool black cherry fruit as well as some rasberry confit. Well measured with lovely precision.

Wine Details

Wine of origin	Swartland
Alcohol level	14.68%
Residual Sugar g/L	3.4
Total Acid g/L	5.72
pH	3.44
Closure type	Cork
Single vineyard	n/a
Grape varietals	Shiraz
Percentage	100%
Irrigated	no
Farm method	n/a
Debut vintage	2011
Total bottles produced	8 094
Approx retail price	R 98

Vinification	Harvested at optimum ripeness, destemmed, gently crushed, fermented in steel. Drained, pressed. Inoculated for MLF. Racked, sterile filtrated, moved to barrels.
Oaking	French oak for 13 months.
Maturation	Racked once after 4 months in oak and aged for another 8 months under strict temperature and humidty control.
Ageing potential	Drink now or store for 2-4 years

Winemaker Notes

Deep purple red, bright hues on rim. Sweet black cherries, red fruit on nose. Fresh juicy blackcurrant, hints of red ruit abound with just enough spice and velvety tannins on the aftertaste.

Producer Details

Vineyard/Producer	Teddy Hall Wines
Physical address	Middebosch, Dorp Street, Stellenbosch
Map page	268-269
GPS co-ordinates	n/a
Established	2005
Owner	Teddy Hall
Cellarmaster	Teddy Hall
Winemaker	Teddy Hall
Viticulturist	Teddy Hall
First bottled vintage	2005
Area under vines	8 ha
Main varieties	Cab Sauv, Syrah, Chen Bl, Chard
Red : white ratio	30 : 70
Total bottle production	200 000

Contact Details

Tel	083 461 8111
Email	teddy@teddyhallwines.com
Web	www.teddyhallwines.com
Tasting days & hours	Closed to public
Tasting fee	n/a
Other attractions	n/a

Personal Tasting Notes

Judges' Comments

Waxy, honeyed richness here with a vibrant zest, pineapple and pear fruit as well as good acidity.

Wine Details

Wine of origin	Stellenbosch
Alcohol level	14.5%
Residual Sugar g/L	5
Total Acid g/L	7
pH	3.23
Closure type	Cork
Single vineyard	Yes
Grape varietals	Chen Bl
Percentage	100%
Irrigated	no
Farm method	n/a
Debut vintage	2008
Total bottles produced	5 000
Approx retail price	R 120

Vinification	Only the free run juice was settled overnight in stainless steel tank. 100% natural fermentation in French oak barriques.
Oaking	French Oak (Vicard Prestige barrels) for 14 months.
Maturation	12 months in French oak barrels, 33% new, 33% 2nd fill and 33% 3rd fill.
Ageing potential	Still young; will drink well between 3-5 years

---

Winemaker Notes

Bright gold, green tinge. Tropical fruit salad nose, pineapple, some quince. On the palate the balance is impeccable with grapefruit, vanilla and baked apple flavours. Long, lingering finish.

Producer Details

Vineyard/Producer	Teddy Hall Wines
Physical address	Middebosch, Dorp Street, Stellenbosch
Map page	268-269
GPS co-ordinates	n/a
Established	2005
Owner	Teddy Hall
Cellarmaster	Teddy Hall
Winemaker	Teddy Hall
Viticulturist	Teddy Hall
First bottled vintage	2005
Area under vines	8 ha
Main varieties	Cab Sauv, Syrah, Chen Bl, Chard
Red : white ratio	30 : 70
Total bottle production	200 000

Contact Details

Tel	083 461 8111
Email	teddy@teddyhallwines.com
Web	www.teddyhallwines.com
Tasting days & hours	Closed to public
Tasting fee	n/a
Other attractions	n/a

Personal Tasting Notes

Judges' Comments

Black fruits, blueberry and some caramel notes with some intense savoury characters as well as fresh fruit.

Wine Details

Wine of origin	Stellenbosch	
Alcohol level	14.5%	
Residual Sugar g/L	1	
Total Acid g/L	6	
pH	37	
Closure type	Cork	
Single vineyard	n/a	
Grape varietals	Cab Sauv	Merl
Percentage	86%	14%
Irrigated	yes	yes
Farm method	n/a	n/a
Debut vintage	2008	
Total bottles produced	600	
Approx retail price	R 350	

Vinification	The cap was punched down 4 times per day. After 7 days of skin contact it was pressed, malolactic fermentation in tank and 14 months in barrel.
Oaking	French oak (Vicard Prestige barrels) for 14 months.
Maturation	As per oaking regime.
Ageing potential	Will gain complexity; will be at its best around 2015

Winemaker Notes

Almost opaque with crimson rim. Nutty and cassis nose with some violets showing. Layered palate, chocolate, blackcurrant and hint of vanilla. Concentration of fruit and complexity seduce.

Producer Details

Vineyard/Producer	Bellingham Wines & Boschendal Wines
Physical address	Boschendal - R310, Pniel Road, Groot Drakenstein
Map page	271
GPS co-ordinates	Boschendal - S 33° 52' 27.5" E 018° 58' 34.4"
Established	n/a
Owner	DGB (Pty) Ltd
Cellarmaster	n/a
Winemaker	JC Bekker (group winemaker)
Viticulturist	Stephan Joubert
First bottled vintage	n/a
Area under vines	n/a
Main varieties	n/a
Red : white ratio	n/a
Total bottle production	n/a

Contact Details

Tel	021 870 4200
Email	vanessas@dgb.co.za
Web	www.dgb.co.za
Tasting days & hours	Boschendal - Mon-Sun 8.30-4.30 (winter), 10-6 (summer)
Tasting fee	Boschendal - R 20 (5 wines), R 30 (conducted tasting)
Other attractions	n/a

Personal Tasting Notes

Judges' Comments

Rich zesty pineapple fruit with notes of citrusy pith and herb. Open apple and pear fruit.

Wine Details

Wine of origin	Coastal
Alcohol level	14%
Residual Sugar g/L	2.1
Total Acid g/L	6.5
pH	3.28
Closure type	Synthetic
Single vineyard	n/a
Grape varietals	Chen Bl
Percentage	100%
Irrigated	yes
Farm method	n/a
Debut vintage	2007
Total bottles produced	33 000
Approx retail price	R 140
Vinification	Hand picked at 23-24° balling, partial whole bunch pressing followed by single lot fermentation.
Oaking	French oak for 9 months.
Maturation	Wine matured in French oak barrels for 9 months. 50% new and 50% 2nd fill French oak.
Ageing potential	3-5 years

Winemaker Notes

Bold layers of tropical fruit and melon follow refreshingly on nose and palate. Subtle sweetness of honeysuckle combines well with fruitiness. Layered, complex wine. Lingering aftertaste.

Producer Details

Vineyard/Producer	The High Road
Physical address	7D Lower Dorp Street, Bosman's Crossing, Stellenbosch
Map page	268-269
GPS co-ordinates	S 33° 56' 27.1" E 018° 50' 49.1"
Established	2003
Owner	Les Sweidan & Mike Church
Cellarmaster	n/a
Winemaker	Mark Carmichael-Green
Viticulturist	Paul Wallace
First bottled vintage	2003
Area under vines	n/a
Main varieties	Cab Sauv, Merl, Cab Fr
Red : white ratio	100% red
Total bottle production	24 000

Contact Details

Tel	076 044 5020
Email	wine@thehighroad.co.za
Web	www.thehighroad.co.za
Tasting days & hours	By appointment
Tasting fee	Complimentary
Other attractions	Pane E Vino Italian restaurant, boardroom facilities

Personal Tasting Notes

Judges' Comments

Sweet berry fruits here alongside some appealing green herbal notes. Rounded and sleek with nice tannic structure. Potential for ageing.

THE HIGH ROAD

DIRECTOR'S RESERVE
2009
STELLENBOSCH

Wine Details

Wine of origin	Stellenbosch		
Alcohol level	14.5%		
Residual Sugar g/L	2.7		
Total Acid g/L	5.6		
pH	3.69		
Closure type	Cork		
Single vineyard	n/a		
Grape varietals	Cab Sauv	Merl	Cab Fr
Percentage	50%	33%	17%
Irrigated	yes	yes	yes
Farm method	n/a	n/a	n/a
Debut vintage	2010		
Total bottles produced	8 200		
Approx retail price	R 240		

Vinification	Picked at optimal ripeness (24.5° balling). Refrigerated overnight. 10+ sorters remove green elements. Crushed and made at award-winning cellar.
Oaking	French oak for 16 months.
Maturation	16 months in new French oak barrels (225L).
Ageing potential	10-15 years

Winemaker Notes

Deep dark ruby centre. Gentle release of vanilla, slight cigar box.
Complex and layered with fruit, wood, dark chocolate nuances.
Blackcurrant and mulberry fruits full on front of palate.

Producer Details

Vineyard/Producer	Tierhoek
Physical address	Tierhoek, Piekenierskloof, Citrusdal
Map page	282
GPS co-ordinates	S 32° 23′ 45.7″ E 018° 51′ 41.2″
Established	2001
Owner	Shelley Sandell
Cellarmaster	Roger Burton
Winemaker	Roger Burton
Viticulturist	Ryno Kellerman
First bottled vintage	2003
Area under vines	16 ha
Main varieties	Chen Bl, Sauv B, Chard, Shiraz, Gren, Mourv
Red : white ratio	50 : 50
Total bottle production	3 000

Contact Details

Tel	021 674 3041
Email	roger@tierhoek.com
Web	www.tierhoek.com
Tasting days & hours	By appointment
Tasting fee	R 20 (waived upon purchase)
Other attractions	Fauna, flora, dam, Sandveld House, mountain biking

Personal Tasting Notes

Judges' Comments

Caremelised barley sugar and honey notes. Sweet and raisined with some syrup notes. Rich and complex.

Wine Details

Wine of origin	Piekenierskloof
Alcohol level	11.5%
Residual Sugar g/L	276
Total Acid g/L	8.6
pH	3.83
Closure type	Cork
Single vineyard	n/a
Grape varietals	Chen Bl
Percentage	100%
Irrigated	no
Farm method	org
Debut vintage	2006
Total bottles produced	120
Approx retail price	R 150
Vinification	Pressed at 40° balling, fermented wild for 6 months in old French oak (225L).
Oaking	60 months in 2nd fill French Barrique.
Maturation	Racked from fermentation barrel then matured in same barrel.
Ageing potential	10-20 years

Winemaker Notes

An unctuous wine of immense concentrated flavours of dried apricots and honey. The sweetness is balanced by a fresh natural fruit acidity leaving a clean finish on the palate

Producer Details

Vineyard/Producer	Tokara
Physical address	Helshoogte Pass, Stellenbosch
Map page	268-269
GPS co-ordinates	S 33° 55′ 06.12″ E 018° 55′ 16.87″
Established	2001
Owner	GT Ferreira
Cellarmaster	Miles Mossop
Winemaker	Miles Mossop
Viticulturist	Aidan Morton
First bottled vintage	2001
Area under vines	105 ha
Main varieties	Sauv B, Chard, Cab Sauv, Shiraz
Red : white ratio	35 : 65
Total bottle production	600 000

Contact Details

Tel	072 227 8274
Email	thelma@tokara.com
Web	www.tokara.com
Tasting days & hours	Mon-Fri 9-5; Sat & Sun 10-4
Tasting fee	Complimentary
Other attractions	Deli, restaurant, oliveshed

Personal Tasting Notes

Judges' Comments

Opulent, ripe style with nicely integrated oak. Good complexity and length with supple, creamy tannins.

Wine Details

Wine of origin	Stellenbosch			
Alcohol level	14.95%			
Residual Sugar g/L	1.4			
Total Acid g/L	0.75			
pH	3.76			
Closure type	Synthetic			
Single vineyard	n/a			
Grape varietals	Cab Sauv	Pet V	Merl	Cab Franc/MerBec
Percentage	73%	15%	6%	6%
Irrigated	yes	yes	yes	yes
Farm method	n/a	n/a	n/a	n/a
Debut vintage	2010			
Total bottles produced	33 000			
Approx retail price	R 248			

Vinification	Destemmed, sorted, crushed. Punch downs, pump overs. Fermented spontaneously. Maceration 16-30 days. Pressed, free run and press wines pumped to barrel for MLF.
Oaking	French oak for 22 months.
Maturation	225L French barrels for 22 months. 6 rackings, blending, light fining, bottling. Blending done through barrel selection.
Ageing potential	10-15 years

Winemaker Notes

Deep, dark, inky garnet colour. Intensely complex. Palate full and rich mirroring the nose with flavours of Christmas cake, cassis and spice, layered with cedar and a eucalyptus finish.

Producer Details

Vineyard/Producer	Tokara
Physical address	Helshoogte Pass, Stellenbosch
Map page	268-269
GPS co-ordinates	S 33° 55′ 06.12″ E 018° 55′ 16.87″
Established	2001
Owner	GT Ferreira
Cellarmaster	Miles Mossop
Winemaker	Miles Mossop
Viticulturist	Aidan Morton
First bottled vintage	2001
Area under vines	105 ha
Main varieties	Sauv B, Chard, Cab Sauv, Shiraz
Red : white ratio	35 : 65
Total bottle production	600 000

Contact Details

Tel	072 227 8274
Email	thelma@tokara.com
Web	www.tokara.com
Tasting days & hours	Mon-Fri 9-5; Sat & Sun 10-4
Tasting fee	Complimentary
Other attractions	Deli, restaurant, oliveshed

Personal Tasting Notes

Judges' Comments

Herbal, lemon meringue, sherbet, limey, tight with slight reduction, ends with a smoky, flinty note and underlying sweetness.

Wine Details

Wine of origin	Stellenbosch	
Alcohol level	13.38%	
Residual Sugar g/L	3.8	
Total Acid g/L	7.5	
pH	3.23	
Closure type	Synthetic	
Single vineyard	n/a	
Grape varietals	Sauv B	Sem
Percentage	70%	30%
Irrigated	yes	yes
Farm method	n/a	n/a
Debut vintage	2010	
Total bottles produced	8 560	
Approx retail price	R 170	

Vinification	Sauv B is a selection from 3 vineyards. Destemmed, crushed, pressed to stainless steel tanks.
Oaking	French oak for 9 months.
Maturation	9 months in barrel on gross lees, regular stirring. Sauv B underwent no MLF while the Sem underwent partial MLF.
Ageing potential	5-8 years

Winemaker Notes

Pale straw colour, tinge of green. Aroma of fresh limes, passion fruit, star fruit. Palate filled with fresh summer fruits. Perfectly integrated oak. Clean, fresh and dry finish.

Producer Details

Vineyard/Producer	Vilafonté
Physical address	Unit 7C, Lower Dorp Street, Bosman's Crossing, Stellenbosch
Map page	268-269
GPS co-ordinates	S 33° 47' 38" E 018° 56' 09"
Established	2003
Owner	Zelma Long, Mike Ratcliffe & Dr. Phillip Freese
Cellarmaster	Martin Smith
Winemaker	Zelma Long
Viticulturist	Dr. Phillip Freese
First bottled vintage	2003
Area under vines	15 ha
Main varieties	Merl, Malb, Cab Sauv, Cab Fr
Red : white ratio	100% red
Total bottle production	16 000

Contact Details

Tel	021 886 4083
Email	sophia@vilafonte.com
Web	www.vilafonte.com
Tasting days & hours	Mon-Fri 9-4 (by appointment)
Tasting fee	R 100 (refunded upon purchase)
Other attractions	n/a

Personal Tasting Notes

Judges' Comments

Modern and direct with rich blackberry and cassis as well as some fresh mineral notes. Masculine and ripe.

Wine Details

Wine of origin	Paarl			
Alcohol level	14.5%			
Residual Sugar g/L	2.4			
Total Acid g/L	6			
pH	3.7			
Closure type	Cork			
Single vineyard	n/a			
Grape varietals	Malb	Merl	Cab Sauv	Cab Fr
Percentage	46%	32%	21%	1%
Irrigated	yes	yes	yes	yes
Farm method	n/a	n/a	n/a	n/a
Debut vintage	2004			
Total bottles produced	8 949			
Approx retail price	R 299			

Vinification	Intensive berry sorting, 5-day cold soak, selected yeast fermentations and careful consideration of phenolic structure in the timing of pressing and extraction.
Oaking	New French oak for 16 months.
Maturation	Barrel ageing for 16 months in new and 2nd fill French oak. 1 year bottle maturation thereafter.
Ageing potential	10 years

Winemaker Notes

A sensuous Malbec and Merlot-styled blend with a firm core structure for ageing. Dark cherry, dark chocolate and fruit cake flavours. Sleek, silky and succulent palate.

Producer Details

Vineyard/Producer	Vondeling
Physical address	Vondeling Farm, Voor Paardeberg
Map page	272-273
GPS co-ordinates	n/a
Established	2001
Owner	Armajaro Estate
Cellarmaster	Matthew Copeland
Winemaker	Matthew Copeland
Viticulturist	Julian Johnsen
First bottled vintage	2004
Area under vines	105 ha
Main varieties	Chen Bl, Chard, Viog, Shiraz, Merl, Cab Sauv
Red : white ratio	60 : 40
Total bottle production	200 000

Contact Details

Tel	021 869 8595
Email	francois@vondelingwines.co.za
Web	www.vondelingwines.co.za
Tasting days & hours	n/a
Tasting fee	n/a
Other attractions	n/a

Personal Tasting Notes

Judges' Comments

Fresh, well-judged oak, nice grippy rasberry fruit here. Bright with a spicy, savoury, mocha twist to the fruit.

2011

VONDELING

BALDRICK SHIRAZ

Wine Details

Wine of origin	Voor Paardeberg		
Alcohol level	14%		
Residual Sugar g/L	4.8		
Total Acid g/L	6.2		
pH	3.51		
Closure type	Screw cap		
Single vineyard	n/a		
Grape varietals	Shiraz	Mourv	Viog
Percentage	90%	9%	1%
Irrigated	yes	yes	yes
Farm method	n/a	n/a	n/a
Debut vintage	2006		
Total bottles produced	25 000		
Approx retail price	R 50		

Vinification	Cool fermentation with hand plunging/mixing allowing the winemaker to produce a more elegant, fruit-driven profile.
Oaking	French oak for 11 months.
Maturation	Older French oak barrels were used for maturation, so as not to over-wood the wine and disrupt the subtle balance.
Ageing potential	8 years

Winemaker Notes

The aromas glide seamlessly through to the finish across a smooth and accessible palate. Simply put, this wine was tailor-made to excite your taste buds.

Producer Details

Vineyard/Producer	Vondeling
Physical address	Vondeling Farm, Voor Paardeberg
Map page	272-273
GPS co-ordinates	n/a
Established	2001
Owner	Armajaro Estate
Cellarmaster	Matthew Copeland
Winemaker	Matthew Copeland
Viticulturist	Julian Johnsen
First bottled vintage	2004
Area under vines	105 ha
Main varieties	Chen Bl, Chard, Viog, Shiraz, Merl, Cab Sauv
Red : white ratio	60 : 40
Total bottle production	200 000

Contact Details

Tel	021 869 8595
Email	francois@vondelingwines.co.za
Web	www.vondelingwines.co.za
Tasting days & hours	n/a
Tasting fee	n/a
Other attractions	n/a

Personal Tasting Notes

Judges' Comments

Fresh and lively with apricot, citrus and melon fruit. Quince and litchi complexity. Perfumed and focussed with lovely balance.

VONDELING

Sweet Carolyn

2007

Wine Details

Wine of origin	Voor Paardeberg
Alcohol level	9.5%
Residual Sugar g/L	178
Total Acid g/L	8.6
pH	3.05
Closure type	Cork
Single vineyard	n/a
Grape varietals	Muscat de Frontignan
Percentage	100%
Irrigated	yes
Farm method	n/a
Debut vintage	2004
Total bottles produced	900
Approx retail price	R 130

Vinification	The grapes are harvested at the same time and placed on beds of straw in our old wooden sheds. The straw helps disperse moisture and prevent rot.
Oaking	French oak for 12 months.
Maturation	The wine is aged for 1 year in old French oak before it is bottled and matured before release.
Ageing potential	50 years

Winemaker Notes

The mouthwatering sweetness is cut by tangy acidity to provide a lingering aftertaste.

Producer Details

Vineyard/Producer	Warwick Wine Estate
Physical address	R44 Road, between Stellenbosch & Klapmuts
Map page	268-269
GPS co-ordinates	S 33° 50' 27" E 018° 51' 54"
Established	1964
Owner	The Ratcliffe Family
Cellarmaster	Nic van Aarde
Winemaker	Nic van Aarde
Viticulturist	Ronald Spies
First bottled vintage	1986
Area under vines	50 ha
Main varieties	Cab Sauv, Cab Fr, Merl, Sauv B, Ptage, Chard
Red : white ratio	60 : 40
Total bottle production	300 000

Contact Details

Tel	021 884 4410
Email	colleen@warwickwine.com
Web	www.warwickwine.com
Tasting days & hours	Mon-Sun 10-5
Tasting fee	R 25
Other attractions	Gourmet picnics, Big 5 vineyard & horseback safaris

Personal Tasting Notes

Judges' Comments

Well balanced, ripe and fruit-forward but with good structure and appealing blackberry, cassis and spicy characters.

WARWICK
— ESTATE —

TRILOGY

2009

STELLENBOSCH SOUTH AFRICA

Wine Details

Wine of origin	Stellenbosch		
Alcohol level	14.26%		
Residual Sugar g/L	2.5		
Total Acid g/L	6.2		
pH	3.64		
Closure type	Cork		
Single vineyard	n/a		
Grape varietals	Cab Sauv	Mourv	Cab Fr
Percentage	60%	11%	29%
Irrigated	yes	yes	yes
Farm method	bio	bio	bio
Debut vintage	1986		
Total bottles produced	31 100		
Approx retail price	R 250		

Vinification	Hand picked early morning. Destemmed, berries sorted on vibrating table. Crushed open slightly, pumped into open-top vats. Variety of yeasts used, daily pump overs.
Oaking	French oak barriques.
Maturation	27 months in 225L French oak barrels (60% new, 20% 2nd, 20% 3rd fill). Blended, light fining, rough filtration. Bottled.
Ageing potential	10-15 years

Winemaker Notes

Displays an intense ruby red colour in the glass. Bouquet is reminiscent of cherries, blackcurrants and has tones of dark chocolate. The palate is full bodied with firm but silky tannins.

Producer Details

Vineyard/Producer	Wildekrans Wine Estate
Physical address	R43, Bot River
Map page	278
GPS co-ordinates	S 34° 14' 28.04" E 019° 12' 50.61"
Established	1993
Owner	Gary Harlow
Cellarmaster	William Wilkinson
Winemaker	William Wilkinson
Viticulturist	Braam Gericke
First bottled vintage	1993
Area under vines	65 ha
Main varieties	Chen Bl, Ptage, Shiraz, Cab Fr, Sauv B, Merl
Red : white ratio	60 : 40
Total bottle production	200 000

Contact Details

Tel	082 658 0009
Email	marelize@wildekrans.com
Web	www.wildekrans.com
Tasting days & hours	Mon-Fri 8.30-4.30; Sat & Sun 11-3
Tasting fee	R 15 for 5 wines
Other attractions	Vineyard & cellar tours

Personal Tasting Notes

Judges' Comments

Bold with a peppermint lift to the exotic quince, melon and pear fruit. Lovely depth of flavour.

BARREL SELECTION
CHENIN BLANC
2010
WINE OF ORIGIN BOT RIVER, SOUTH AFRICA

Wine Details

Wine of origin	Bot River
Alcohol level	14.56%
Residual Sugar g/L	4.2
Total Acid g/L	6.6
pH	3.5
Closure type	Cork
Single vineyard	n/a
Grape varietals	Chen Bl
Percentage	100%
Irrigated	yes
Farm method	bio
Debut vintage	2011
Total bottles produced	1 200
Approx retail price	R 120

Vinification	Early morning harvest from 30-year-old vines. Hand picked at 25° balling. Only free run juice was used.
Oaking	New French oak for 12 months.
Maturation	Fermented in 300L/400L French oak barrels.
Ageing potential	5-7 years

Winemaker Notes

Golden glow, pale straw shine. Slightly citrusy showing subtle peach with the warm undertones of almond on the nose. Finish of apricot, vanilla and grapefruit with a hint of honey.

PORTFOLIO

www.portfoliocollection.com

A Collection of Portfolio's hand-picked and benchmarked Private Game Reserves, Lodges Country Houses, Boutique Hotels, Retreats ity Guest Houses, Villas, Apartments, Farm Stays and Bed & Breakfasts including Township B&Bs in South Africa, Namibia and Swaziland

2012

log:
avelblog.portfoliocollection.com/
acebook:
ww.facebook.com/PortfolioCollectionSA
witter
witter.com/PortfolioSA

Benchmark of the Best for 30 Years
THE INFORMED CHOICE FOR THE INDEPENDENT TRAVELLER

Wine is an integral part of any good dining experience. Fine wines and great service are both key to enhancing a great dining experience.

Restaurant owners and managers correctly believe that their customers deserve to have access to a high-integrity wine list with a well-chosen range of choices that pair well with the menu. Diners and wine lovers alike regularly seek an independently reviewed and highly regarded wine list. Thus, both restaurateurs and their customers benefit from the plausible Quality Awards and rankings as well as from the Best Value Awards for winning establishments. These underpin the enhancement of their overall dining enjoyment.

More international travellers seeking a fine wine and dine set of experiences are visiting South Africa. They have reasonable expectations for better quality wine and service. Locals too are voicing their needs and desires in a similar fashion. The annual **Top 100 SA Wine List Challenge** will help to fulfil these important needs. The Challenge is a premier judged event held in Cape Town, South Africa and provides restaurants with the opportunity to enter their wine lists. It is open to all establishments in South Africa. The objective is simple – identify South Africa's best wine lists in a ranked manner and make these facts available.

The Wine List Challenge provides an independent, objective and professional rating of all entered wine lists. The expert panel consists of some of the most highly regarded South African consulting sommeliers.

It is not necessary for establishments to have a huge wine position in order to do well in the Challenge. There are many ways in which to make the wine proposition for diners extremely enjoyable without massive investment. Patrons value care and thought. Having said this, of course it may be very desirable to have a world-class wine list that competes with the absolute best. Realistically this is not something that every establishment can afford or, indeed, might want.

Wine lovers are in for yet another accessible treat. Top 100 now offers private fine-dining events together with paired wines where you will meet the acclaimed winemaker. Entertaining as well as a learning opportunity, these will be available at a limited number of great restaurants throughout the year. Auslese in Cape Town and Rodwell House are both organising a programme for 2012. Other select restaurants will offer you similar local opportunities shortly.

The methodology applied to assess and rate wine lists is based on research conducted in Europe and the USA on best practice. These were then remodelled to provide the template below which has been summarised for ease of reference.

QUALITY AWARD SCORING METHODOLOGY (100 POINTS)

- Presentation: physical, layout, description (8)
- Wine service, with additional points for qualified or unqualified sommelier (14)
- South African content: depth, breadth & balance (30)
- International content: depth, breadth & balance (12)
- Glassware: quality, range and setting (10)
- Food and wine pairing (5)
- Unusual bottle sizes (12)
- BYO clarity (4)
- Cellaring and cellar conditions (5)

BEST VALUE AWARD SCORING METHODOLOGY (100 POINTS)

Bottles

- Seven red wines listed at under R150 per bottle (28)
- Seven white/rosé wines under R150 per bottle (28)
- One MCC under R200 per bottle (4)
- Two red wines listed under R110 per bottle (8)
- Two white wines listed under R110 per bottle (8)

Wines by the glass

- Two white wines at under R35 per glass (8)
- Two red wines at under R35 per glass (8)
- One MCC at under R40 per glass (4)

Special offers or bin-end sales

- There needs to be evidence of special offers that are discounted (4)

Mark-up percentage: the wines above should be marked up from Trade Cost at no more than 130% net of VAT.

Judging Process

- Five Quality Award judges and three Best Value Award judges assessed.
- Judges are independent and answered to the Chair.
- Wine lists were sighted; judges' interests were pre-recorded.
- No judge with an establishment relationship could judge that establishment.
- All contended wine lists were assessed by the panel plus Chair.
- The Chair had a casting vote.

Quality Awards

For the 2012 Wine List challenge, there were four levels of awards based on level of quality. These four levels are indicated below, together with the required level of points scored out of 100 in order to earn the award:

- Inspirational (91-100/100 points)
- Outstanding (66-90/100 points)
- Excellent (41-65/100 points)
- Highly Regarded (30-40/100 points)

Best Value Awards

- Professional judges nominated wine lists for possible Best Value Awards.
- A minimum Quality Award score of 40/100 was the requirement to be eligible for a Best Value Award.
- A Best Value score of 80+/100 was required to win an award.
- A separate Consumer Panel of judges assessed these lists for possible nomination.
- Overall value is the key criteria: can consumers buy good or very good wines at attractive prices by the glass, bottle or even by the magnum?
- These awards can be earned in addition to the Quality Awards.

Jörg Pfützner – Chair of both panels

QUALITY AWARDS

Higgo Jacobs

Mia Martensson

Kent Scheermeyer

Jenny Ratcliffe-Wright

BEST VALUE AWARDS

Dax Villanueva

Maryna Strachan

Harry Haddon

Inspirational (91-100 points)
96 Winery Road* (Stellenbosch)
Aubergine Restaurant (Cape Town)
Bosman's Restaurant (Paarl)
Restaurant Mosaic* (Pretoria)
Reuben's (Cape Town)

Outstanding (66-90 points)
Azure Restaurant (Cape Town)
Bushmans Kloof Wilderness Reserve and Wellness Retreat (Clanwilli
Capelands Restaurant Mangiare* (Somerset West)
French Toast Wine & Tapas Bar (Cape Town)
Karibu Restaurant* (Cape Town)
Kitima at the Kronendal* (Cape Town)
The Grill Room (Umhlanga)
Zachary's Restaurant (Knysna)

Excellent (41-66 points)
Bientang's Cave Restaurant* (Hermanus)
Blue Water Café* (Cape Town)
Café del Sol* (Johannesburg)
Dear Me (Cape Town)
Fishmonger Centurion* (Pretoria)
Hemingways Restaurant and Wine Cellar* (Pretoria)
Pigalle Restaurant Sandton (Johannesburg)
Pride of India (Pretoria)
Prosopa Restaurant* (Pretoria)
Reuben's Restaurant & Bar (Franschhoek)
The Raj Indian Restaurant (Johannesburg)
Verdicchio Restaurant & Wine Cellar* (Johannesburg)

Highly Regarded (30-40 points)
Arpeggio Ristoranté (Stellenbosch)
La Pentola (Pretoria)
Pigalle Restaurant Bedfordview (Johannesburg)
Pigalle Restaurant Melrose Arch (Johannesburg)
Sofia's at Morgenster (Somerset West)
TSG 4Ways Mediterranean Grill Café (Johannesburg)
Zinzi Restaurant (Plettenberg Bay)

* indicates restaurant achieved a Best Value Award.

EASTERN CAPE

Zachary's Restaurant

Outstanding

Web: www.pezula.com

Email: info@zacharys.co.za

Phone: 044 302 3364

Address: Duthie Drive, Knysna

Cooking / Menu Style: Clean, honest approach to food, with a unique style.

EASTERN CAPE

Zinzi Restaurant

Highly Regarded

Web: www.hunterhotels.com

Email: zinzi@hunterhotels.com

Phone: 044 532 8226

Address: Tsala Treetop Lodge, Harkerville, Hunter's Estate off N2, 10km W of Plett

Cooking / Menu Style: Authentic culture, contemporary cool. Primarily North African flavours.

GAUTENG

Café del Sol

Excellent

Web: www.cafedelsol.co.za

Email: info@cafedelsol.co.za

Phone: 011 704 6493

Address: Corner Shopping Centre, cnr Olive & President Fouche Roads, Olivedale, JHB

BEST VALUE AWARD SA WINES

Cooking / Menu Style: New-age Italian family sharing delightful food cooked with love and integrity.

GAUTENG

Pigalle Restaurant – Bedfordview

Highly Regarded

Web: www.pigallerestaurants.co.za

Email: bedford@pigallerestaurants.co.za

Phone: 011 450 2242

Address: Shop 36 Village View Shop Ctr, cnr Kloof & van Buuren Rd, Bedfordview, JHB

Cooking / Menu Style: Seafood and shellfish dishes; a focus on Portuguese-inspired cuisine.

Pigalle Restaurant – Melrose Arch
Highly Regarded
Web: www.pigallerestaurants.co.za
Email: melrose@pigallerestaurants.co.za
Phone: 011 684 2711
Address: Shop HL48 Level 05 / Orange Melrose Arch, Corlett Drive, Melrose, JHB
Cooking / Menu Style: Shellfish grilled to longstanding recipe; speciality meat and poultry dishes.

Pigalle Restaurant – Sandton
Excellent
Web: www.pigallerestaurants.co.za
Email: sandton@pigallerestaurants.co.za
Phone: 011 884 8899
Address: Shop U09, 4th Floor, Michelangelo Towers, Maude Street, Sandton, JHB
Cooking / Menu Style: Sensational menu including impeccably prepared meat, fish and poultry dishes.

The Raj Indian Restaurant
Excellent
Web: www.theraj.co.za
Email: info@theraj.co.za
Phone: 011 468 1861
Address: Crowthorne Shopping Centre, cnr Main and Arthur Roads, Kyalami, JHB
Cooking / Menu Style: Indian cuisine.

TSG 4Ways Mediterranean Grill Café
Highly Regarded
Web: www.tsg4ways.co.za
Email: info@tsg4ways.co.za
Phone: 011 465 7270
Address: The Leaping Frog Garden Centre, cnr William Nicol Drive & Mulbarton Road, Fourways, JHB
Cooking / Menu Style: Italian with a South African twist.

GAUTENG
**Verdicchio Restaurant
and Wine Cellar**
Excellent

Web: www.verdicchio.co.za
Email: verdicchio@mweb.co.za
Phone: 011 511 1969
Address: Shop 9 Montecasino, Fourways, JHB

Cooking / Menu Style: A venue for superior traditional Italian food.

GAUTENG
Fishmonger Centurion
Excellent
Web: n/a
Email: fishmonger@iburst.co.za
Phone: 012 643 1429
Address: Centurion Gate Centre, John Vorster Drive, Centurion,
Pretoria
Cooking / Menu Style: Seafood restaurant.

GAUTENG
Hemingways Restaurant & Cellar
Excellent

Web: www.hemingwaysrestaurant.co.za
Email: sales@leriba.co.za / chef@leriba.co.za
Phone: 012 660 3300
Address: Leriba Hotel & Spa, 245 End Street,
Clubview, Centurion, Pretoria
Cooking / Menu Style: The classical, contemporary and
cosmopolitan dishes are honest and adventurous.

GAUTENG
La Pentola
Highly Regarded
Web: www.lapentola.co.za
Email: us@lapentola.co.za
Phone: 012 329 4028
Address: Shop 5, Well Street, Riviera, Pretoria

Cooking / Menu Style: French, Italian and Mediterranean.

GAUTENG

Pride of India
Excellent
Web: http://www.dining-out.co.za/
member_details-MemberID-1982.html
Email: kbhima@worldonline.co.za
Phone: 012 346 3684
Address: 22 Groenkloof Plaza, 43 George
Storrar Drive, Groenkloof, Pretoria
Cooking / Menu Style: Fine-dining Indian cuisine.

GAUTENG

Prosopa Restaurant
Excellent

Web: http://www.wininganddining.co.za/
gauteng/pretoria/waterkloof-heights/
prosopa
Email: dino@prosopa.co.za
Phone: 012 460 1663
Address: Waterkloof Heights Centre, 103 Club Ave, Pretoria
Cooking / Menu Style: Mediterranean, Greek, Portuguese.

GAUTENG

Restaurant Mosaic
Inspirational
Web: www.restaurantmosaic.com
Email: reservations@restaurantmosaic.com
Phone: 012 371 2902
Address: The Orient Boutique Hotel,
Francolin Conservation Area, Elandsfontein,
Crocodile River Valley, Pretoria
Cooking / Menu Style: A mosaic of classical cuisine innovation.

KWA-ZULU NATAL

The Grill Room
Outstanding
Web: www.oysterboxhotel.com/dining
Email: restaurants@oysterbox.co.za
Phone: 031 514 5000
Address: 2 Lighthouse Road, Umhlanga
Rocks
Cooking / Menu Style: Tasteful, ethnically inspired menus.
Perfection for the palate.

WESTERN CAPE

Aubergine Restaurant

Inspirational

Web: www.aubergine.co.za

Email: info@aubergine.co.za

Phone: 021 465 4909

Address: 39 Barnet Street, Gardens,
Cape Town

Cooking / Menu Style: Classical foundation with influences from the East and West.

WESTERN CAPE

Azure Restaurant

Outstanding

Web: www.12apostleshotel.com/dining/
dining/azure

Email: azure@12apostles.co.za

Phone: 021 437 9029

Address: Victoria Road, Camps Bay,
Cape Town

Cooking / Menu Style: Indigenous and international cuisine.

WESTERN CAPE

Blue Water Café

Excellent

Web: www.bluewatercafe.co.za

Email: info@bluewatercafe.co.za

Phone: 021 783 2007

Address: Imhoff Farm, Kommetjie Road,
Kommetjie, Cape Town

Cooking / Menu Style: New Cape style and pizzas.

WESTERN CAPE

Dear Me

Excellent

Web: www.dearme.co.za

Email: info@dearme.co.za

Phone: 021 422 4920

Address: 165 Longmarket Street, Cape Town

Cooking / Menu Style: Simple and honest food saturated with love and respect.

French Toast Wine & Tapas Bar
Outstanding
Web: www.frenchtoastwine.com
Email: info@frenchtoastwine.com
Phone: 021 422 3839
Address: 199 Bree Street, Cape Town

Cooking / Menu Style: Tapas and Mediterranean.

Karibu Restaurant
Outstanding
Web: www.kariburestaurant.co.za
Email: kariburestaurant@mweb.co.za
Phone: 021 421 7005/6
Address: Shop 156, The Wharf Centre,
V & A Waterfront, Cape Town

Cooking / Menu Style: Afrikaans, Cape Malay.

Kitima at the Kronendal
Outstanding
Web: www.kitima.co.za
Email: reservations@kitima.co.za
Phone: 021 790 8004
Address: 140 Main Road, Hout Bay,
Cape Town

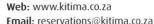

Cooking / Menu Style: Asian cuisine prepared by 5-star Thai chefs.

Reuben's at One & Only
Inspirational
Web: http://capetown.oneandonlyresorts.
com/cuisine/reubens.aspx
Email: restaurant.reservations@
oneandonlycapetown.com
Phone: 021 431 4511
Address: Dock Road, V & A Waterfront, Cape Town
Cooking / Menu Style: Deceptively simple wholesome bistro fare;
exciting combination of local flavours.

WESTERN CAPE
Bushmans Kloof
Outstanding
Web: www.bushmanskloof.co.za
Email: info@bushmanskloof.co.za
Phone: 021 481 1860
Address: Cederberg Mountains,
40km from Clanwilliam

Cooking / Menu Style: Contemporary; fusion of healthy country food and sensational gourmet fare.

WESTERN CAPE
Reuben's Restaurant & Bar
Excellent
Web: www.reubens.co.za
Email: reubens@mweb.co.za
Phone: 021 876 3772
Address: 19 Huguenot Street, Franschhoek

Cooking / Menu Style: Offers favourites as well as specials that are updated daily.

WESTERN CAPE
Bientang's Cave Restaurant
Excellent

BEST
VALUE
AWARD
SA WINES

Web: www.bientangscave.com
Email: bientang@whalemail.co.za
Phone: 028 312 3454
Address: Below Marine Drive (100m from
Old Harbour), Hermanus

Cooking / Menu Style: Various seafood and daily specials; delectable desserts and coffees.

WESTERN CAPE
Bosman's Restaurant
Inspirational
Web: www.granderoche.com/dining.html
Email: reserve@grandroche.co.za
Phone: 021 863 5100
Address: The Grand Roche, Plantasie
Street, Paarl

Cooking / Menu Style: Infusion of classical international cuisine with imagination and innovation.

WESTERN CAPE

**Capelands Restaurant
Mangiare**
Outstanding
Web: www.capelands.com
Email: restaurant@capelands.com
Phone: 021 858 1477
Address: 3 Old Sir Lowry's Pass Road,
Somerset West

Cooking / Menu Style: Mediterranean-style cooking.

WESTERN CAPE

Sofia's at Morgenster
Highly Regarded
Web: http://www.morgenster.co.za/
Restaurant.php
Email: sofiasatmorgenster@gmail.com
Phone: 021 847 1993
Address: Morgenster Estate, Vergelegen

Avenue (off Lourensford Road), Somerset West
Cooking / Menu Style: Classic dishes given a modern twist.

WESTERN CAPE

96 Winery Road
Inspirational
Web: www.96wineryroad.co.za
Email: wineryrd@mweb.co.za
Phone: 021 842 2020
Address: Winery Road, Zandberg Farm,
Stellenbosch

Cooking / Menu Style: Inspired by South African favourites and
flavours from around the world.

WESTERN CAPE

Arpeggio Ristoranté
Highly Regarded
Web: www.arpeggio.co.za
Email: info@arpeggio.co.za
Phone: 021 883 9623
Address: Corner of Church & Mill streets,
Stellenbosch

Cooking / Menu Style: High-quality authentic Italian food.

auslese
sophisticated wines

Auslese is the specialised wine and food pairing venue of Aubergine Restaurant's Harald Bresselschmidt. Designed for exclusive functions and winemaker's dinners, Auslese offers:

- tailor made pairing menus
- impeccable wine service
- fine wines cellared in optimum conditions
- a sumptuous gastronomic experience

Experience firsthand explanations from the winemaker and chef. Host your own event or attend a Top 100 SA Wines dinner with one of the outstanding producers represented in this guide.

www.auslese.co.za • info@auslese.co.za • 115 hope street gardens • cape town • +27(0)21 461 9727

BISTRO

MODERN MEDITERRANEAN
IN-SEASON CUISINE

A LA CARTE FINE DINING AL FRESCO

Superb sea-views, relaxed ambiance, beautiful gardens,
delicious in-season cuisine, award-winning wine-list

Perfect venue for small intimate functions

OPENING HOURS:
Breakfast 08:30 - 11:30, Lunch 12:00 - 15:00, Dinner 18:30 - 22:00
(CLOSED SUNDAY DINNER)

BOOKINGS 021 787 9880

RODWELL HOUSE

HOUSED AT RODWELL HOUSE
RODWELL ROAD . ST JAMES . CAPE TOWN . SOUTH AFRICA
INFO@RODWELLHOUSE.CO.ZA WWW.RODWELLHOUSE.CO.ZA

One&Only
Cape Town

BLENDED WHITES: THE CAPE'S MOST EXCITING WINE STYLE?

Ask a group of South Africans to name their country's outstanding wine style and I suspect you'd get a spread of votes. That's democracy, after all. There'd be a few fringe candidates – the odd fortified, a sweet wine or two, even (for the controversially minded) the occasional Pinotage – but the consensus would probably favour one of two red categories: Shiraz and red blends.

My hunch is that very few locals would pick a dry white wine. This despite the fact that the Cape makes some very good examples of Chardonnay, Sauvignon Blanc and especially Chenin Blanc, the last in a range of styles that are unique and produced, in many cases, from old vines. Indeed, outside South Africa, I'd argue that the country's whites are rated more highly than its reds.

Call me perverse, but my own choice would be a Cape white blend, combining two or more of the following varieties: Chenin (of course), Chardonnay, Verdelho, Viognier, Marsanne, Roussanne, Grenache Blanc, Clairette, Semillon and Sauvignon Blanc. As a serious category, I'd argue that this has emerged in the last decade and is still in its infancy. Blended wines aren't always an easy sell – people prefer the safety and the does-what-it-says-on-the-label certainty of varietals – but they are fast becoming some of the New World's most distinctive whites.

The "Bordeaux-style" blends produced by the likes of Tokara, Flagstone and Cape Point are brilliant and wouldn't look out of place in Pessac-Léognan, but what might be termed the Rhône and Mediterranean-style whites (and yes, I know that Chenin doesn't belong in either place) are arguably even more exciting.

The father (Eben Sadie is too young to be a grandfather of anything) of them all is Sade Family's Palladius, surely the Cape's most ambitious white wine, but I love the blends made by Rall Wines, David Mullineux and Fable, too.

Ten years from now, my prediction is that Cape white blends will be a much bigger category. What's more, I think they will be recognised as a set of innovative, world-class wines. In the meantime, let's enjoy what the pioneers are producing: distinctive blends of real personality.

Tim Atkin MW

Until the mid-1990s, every bottle of wine was sealed the same way. With a cork. The bark of cork oaks is unusual in that it is quite spongy and compressible, but has an elastic memory. This means it does a good job of being compressed into a bottleneck, and then holding its seal well for many years.

But cork has a problem. As a natural product it is variable, and after many years bottles of the same wine all have slightly different characters. And worse still, a small proportion of wines are spoiled by a musty taint that is produced by microbes growing in the tiny holes in the cork (the cork washing and production process will have removed the microbes, but the taint, caused by the chemical trichloroanisole, remains). This is what is known as corked wine, and it's why restaurants ask guests to taste a sample of the wine.

Because of these problems, alternatives were sought. In the mid-1990s the first challenger to cork's crown was the synthetic (plastic) cork. The early versions were difficult to extract from the bottle and it turned out that they didn't protect the wine very well from oxygen. Even though these synthetic corks sealed the bottles tightly, enough oxygen diffused in to give the wines quite a short shelf life. Modern synthetic corks are much better, but they are not suitable for wines destined for long cellaring.

Then, in 2000, the Australians began championing screw caps and were rapidly joined by the New Zealanders. In the past, people had been worried about the image of screw caps and their potential association with cheap wine. But the closure rapidly grew in popularity. Screw caps are incredibly convenient to use – you don't need a tool to open the bottle – and because they protect the wine from oxygen, bottles sealed this way stay fresher for longer.

It is now becoming clear that the closure used has the potential to change the way the wine tastes in subtle ways. Many winemakers choose the closure to suit the wine styles. Some red wines simply taste better when they are sealed with a cork; crisp, fruity whites seem to taste better when screw capped. It's a complex subject, and some of the science of what happens to a wine after it is bottled is still poorly understood. In the meantime, it looks like different wines sealed differently is here to stay.

Jamie Goode

THE PERILS OF WINE
TRANSPORTATION AND SHIPPING

To evolve into something alluring, wine undergoes various chemical and biological reactions in bottle. In order to effect this change, wine must be kept under the correct conditions, optimally 12-16°C. Unfortunately, I still taste wines adversely affected by excessive heat showing cooked aromas, oxidised flavours and dull fruit. My first instinct is to question winemaking practices. However, modern winemakers are fastidious in monitoring temperature in their grapes and wine. Common practices include picking in the early morning coolness, fermenting at low temperatures to preserve esters and, post-bottling, using regulated air-conditioned premises to warehouse the wine. But what about shipping practices?

On leaving the winery, palletised wine is packed into metal containers, superb conductors of heat. All European-destined containers are uninsulated with only 2% making use of thermal linings. At the dockside, containers can regularly reach 45°-60°C. On-board ship, containers can be placed next to the ship's boilers, on the deck in full sunlight or, preferably, in the ship's bowels. As wine is not considered a perishable food, flowers and fresh fruit get prime position. Discharging of containers at the destination and customs clearance mean containers stand in uninsulated warehouses for up to a week before delivery to the distributors.

Clearly, wine transportation is a weak link in keeping wine intact and producers often recant stories about problems they have encountered with heat-affected wines. Despite this, few take any measures to insulate the wine, rendering it ironic having taken so much trouble during the winemaking process to do just that. Although it is unfair to say producers are apathetic to their wine's onward journey, 99% of wine is sent Free on Board, which means once the wine has left their premises it becomes the responsibility of the buyer. Sadly, though, the consumer on opening a bottle of prematurely aged wine lays the blame at the producer's feet resulting in potential lost future purchases. Consumers should pressurise producers and buyers to build in costs for thermal insulation and persuade producers and freight forwarders to get shippers to change their practices in treating wine like a food. This will be one step toward ensuring more sound wine, a winning situation for us all.

Richard Kershaw MW

FROM ONE ARTIST TO ANOTHER,

Congratulations to all of the Top 100 winemakers for 2012.

THE GRAPHIC BALLROOM
DESIGN STUDIO

proud designers of the **TOP 100 SA WINE GUIDE.**

www.gbr.co.za

For many North Americans, wine is fast becoming part of the culture and the regular dinner table. Unlike most of their parents, this generation is better equipped to buy it, cellar it, discuss it and drink it than ever before. Their curiosity about wine and the ability to research instantly with their favourite hand-held device is something every wine producer in South Africa should note.

It is no longer adequate to simply be open for business or boast an attractive tasting room. Strange as it may sound, more than ever it is all about the wine. I know, how dare consumers demand better wine! The nerve of this next generation, wanting a more meaningful story, less pretension, and wine that tastes like it was made by someone and comes from somewhere. Oh, and value too? There is no timetable for this kind of change in the wine business. Patience is required to make meaningful alterations, but there is little doubt the day of the 95-point oak bomb full of overripe, sweet fruit and hard tannins is finally coming to an end. I can only point to some of the more extraordinary on-site tastings I have experienced recently in Bierzo, Spain, Alto Cachapoal, Chile and Alto-Adige, Italy. Each represents an eye-opening shift in wine growing and wine styles. Fresher, brighter, more electric wines directly connected to their unique terroir. To that end, I suggest varietal wine is losing its grip on the modern drinker. When you think about it, Cabernet, Chardonnay and Shiraz come with so much baggage it's a miracle they made it this far down the wine road. Do you really want your Syrah compared with far-flung examples in Argentina? Your Sauvignon Blanc measured against New Zealand? Or would you rather celebrate your dry-farmed, bush vines red blends from Paardeberg that cannot be replicated in the Napa or Barossa valleys.

The French are the masters of terroir-based wine, probably because they concluded a long time ago that no one can copy place. It is why varietal Sauvignon Blanc from Chile doesn't scare the folks in Sancerre. On the other hand, Leyda Sauvignon Blanc from Chile or Hermanus Chardonnay are a much different story. Wines from real, specific places are formidable foes. In the new world of wine, it's all about people and place. But come to think of it, that's what the old world of wine is about, too.

Anthony Gismondi

Asian cuisine is one of the most loved food styles all over the world. It has become so popular and expanded widely, so it's now not difficult to enjoy Asian food almost anywhere worldwide, no matter where you are.

Many unique sauces are used in Asian cuisine and form the basis of most dishes. One of the most popular is soy sauce, but there are also many sauces, commonly known as fish sauce, made from fermented fish and shellfish layered in salt. These include *ishiru* in Japan, *nam pla* in Thailand and *nouc mam* in Vietnam. In China, you find XO sauce (spicy, seafood paste) made from dried shrimp, scallop and high quality ham. These special sauces and pastes have flourished widely in our cuisine. An important element in refined Japanese cuisine is a special soup called Dashi, made from extracts of seaweed, bonito flakes and Shiitake mushrooms. Most white wines strongly emphasise the iodine seawater flavour of these seafood-based dishes and sometimes non-Asians feel that this pairing is too strong for them. The strong fruitiness of most New World red wines is too excessive for most Asian savoury dishes. However, South African reds often show savouriness on the palate, so these exhibit a good pairing with our savoury dishes.

Few South African wines are imported into Japan, so it is rare to taste these here. But it's easy to identify them during blind tastings, due to their 'savoury' taste. This is particularly true of Sauvignon Blanc and Cabernet Sauvignon, Pinotage, and sometimes Syrah. The complex taste of high-quality South African wines always enhances the umami taste evident in savoury Asian dishes and works in wonderful harmony.

For me personally, a memorable experience was a dish of Yellowtail Teriyaki (grilled with sweet soy sauce), which was absolutely beautifully accompanied by two bottles of elderly Pinotage, one from Simonsig and one from Rijks. Their gorgeous fruitiness offered the perfect balance to match the sweet and savoury Yellowtail. Sauvignon Blanc is my suggestion if people would like to enjoy the Vietnamese dish of spring rolls flavoured with coriander leaves. The leafy complexity tasted on the mid-palate in this variety will accompany the strong herbal taste of the sweet and savoury sauce. Through these suggestions, I would like to be a bridge of eating and drinking cultures across the world, as someone from Japan who is actively involved in the wine world.

Kenichi Ohashi

In most cases, the price and quality of a wine are not directly related. In basic terms, it costs a similar amount to produce a bottle of expensive or inexpensive wine (give or take a few factors), and it is the branding and marketing that makes up most of the rest of the price. While brands are all important in today's consumer-driven markets, they should still price themselves relative to their quality. Why is it that every time an investment banker or celebrity launches a wine brand, it shoots the lights out in terms of price? It's a bit like the emperor's new clothes – no one will dare even talk about the quality of such a famous wine. If it's expensive, it must be good.

A wine that shows true quality (and also usually shows its terroir) is a beautiful thing. In many cases the price of those iconic quality wines have remained fairly consistent over their long history with price increments that are related to inflation. But no matter how much those wines charge, it is always sheer drinking pleasure. So that brings us to the point of value. It doesn't really matter how much you pay for a wine, as long as it over-delivers in your glass. The person who just paid over the odds for the celebrity wine, but who is well pleased with its status, has received value from the wine, although not in the way the winemaker intended.

Similarly, is the BOGOF (buy one get one free) at the supermarket really the value you think it is when you end up drinking both bottles on one night, since they tasted of absolutely nothing anyway, and you end up having an axe through your head the next day? Essentially, value is very subjective and until consumers are able to sort the wood from the trees themselves, many inferior wines will continue to succeed in the marketplace.

Jenny Ratcliffe-Wright CWM

South Africa, I believe, is in the process of discovering itself, not only in terms of new areas but also the value of old vines in established areas. The potential is mind-blowing. Slowly, producers with savvy are starting to see the benefit of focusing and developing an identity, not only for areas but also for themselves. Styles are becoming more interesting and more international while remaining true to terrior. Passionate winemakers, the unlocking of new sites, and one of the most beautiful viticulture regions in the world all come together to provide a fantastic base from which to work.

While all the potential exists, I do feel we are yet to unlock it on the broader scale. A number of old and new producers continue to push the boundaries and fly the flag, yet the success of brand SA lies in the buy-in of the industry as a whole. Thinking out of the box in terms of viticultural techniques, varieties and interesting sites is essential going forward. We have so many incredible locations only just being explored, while traditional producing areas such as Stellenbosch and Constantia are constantly being reinvented with new pockets or old parcels of vines. The one-stop wine shop concept is slowly being replaced with producers that choose to focus on certain styles and varieties, and one is beginning to see areas becoming synonymous with more focused offerings such as the Swartland, Elgin or Constantia for example. Old vines are slowly receiving more attention as they should thanks to the efforts of a few key individuals and the results are extremely promising. Winemaking techniques and palates are constantly being fine-tuned which, along with the new enthusiasm and passion being injected into the training institutions, is very positive.

As producers gain more perspective in terms of what is actually possible and fine-tune styles and varietal offerings, so the results will follow and South Africa will take its place amongst the fine-wine producing countries. In short, the world of wine needs to watch this space. We are producing some cracking wines at present and I believe that with a bit more self-belief the best is yet to come!

Duncan Savage

The global consumer demand for the finest wines from the greatest wine regions has never been more vibrant. Not even the financial crash of 2008 managed to permanently dampen the insatiable demand for the very finest French Bordeaux and Burgundy, Italy's super Tuscans and Piedmont reds, and California's iconic Napa Valley Cabernets. However, some New World countries have encountered challenges in recent times. Australia's boutique regional wineries have suffered falling export demand due to the prolonged strength of the Aussie dollar and a reduced ability of Australian producers to connect with maturing consumers trading up from the fruit bomb Jacob's Creek style of wines. But how have South Africa and its top producers fared?

Once the so-called 'post apartheid' new kid on the wine block, South Africa's producers have matured and grown in self confidence since the mid-1990s and are no longer grasping out for international inspiration to establish their identity and intrinsic worth. Confidence and flair abound, growing out of the realisation that South Africa's vinous destiny lies primarily in the production and promotion of high-quality fine wines, not mass-produced, confected and constructed brands. The new generation of South African winemaker now attempts to consume some of the finest examples of red Bordeaux, Loire Chenin Blanc, Burgundy and Northern Rhône Hermitage and Côte Rôtie Syrah on a daily basis. This knowledge has inspired confidence. Producers now know where in the quality and stylistic hierarchy their wines fit. But more importantly, their obsessive ambition to improve their own wines so as to be able to place them on the 'top table' with their international contemporaries has resulted in new quality benchmarks being set.

South Africa's fine wines are no longer the most affordable best kept secrets. Consumers globally are embracing their unique style of Old World classicism and structure combined with New World fruit expression. Everyone should expect and accept that demand for South Africa's top wines such as MR de Compostella, A.A.Badenhorst Family Wines, Cape Point Vineyards, Saronsberg, Cederberg, and Klein Constantia, along with other past Top 100 SA Wine winners, will continue to grow, making them increasingly difficult to purchase.

Thankfully, wine guides such as Top 100 SA Wines are out there introducing and guiding consumers to some of the latest and greatest premium wines being made in South Africa.

Greg Sherwood MW

The current global health trend is here to stay and various diets have become part of daily life. Health gurus guide us in what to eat and drink with red wines often referred to as the safe choice as they are fermented to dryness. But are you really turning down the right wines?

If offered a choice of dry or off-dry Riesling, many would choose the dry version as sweetness in white wines is often pointed out as the choice of the uneducated wine drinker. Many sweet wines of outstanding quality and great historic importance are losing ground due to the banning of sugar in our diets. We insist on white wines being classified according to its level of sweetness but how many reds are we seeing with an indication of sweetness level on the label? The question is whether a Primitivo from Puglia or Zinfandel from California will sell as well with an "off-dry" indication on the front label. Zinfandel struggles with uneven ripening which results in green unripe berries mixed in the same cluster as raisins. With the popularity of Californian "Zin", it does not need to go through a costly sorting process as its flaws can be hidden with the help of sweet and clumsy caramel fudge-tasting must concentrate giving it a sugar boost while increasing consumer friendliness.

An Appassimento boom has hit many markets, especially the Nordics. Wines made from semi-dried grapes from Italy's Veneto and Puglia with a name tweak on the label relating to the method of dried grapes being used in the production of the wine, such as Appassimento, Passo, Passitivo, Ripasso, is a success story. Amarone, the king of the semi-dried raisined grapes, has become a brand in itself. There are many Amarone of extraordinary quality which are almost totally dry but the boost in depressingly low-quality price-fighter labels (nicely camouflaged by high alcohol and evident sweetness) threatens the image of the real quality Amarone. Could this trend be related to the tradition of consuming mulled wine, very sweet with the taste of raisins and spices, during the cold winter months? When is the consumer going to start questioning sweetness levels of 10-20 grams of sugar per litre in red wines?

Maybe it's not so bad after all to enjoy a glass of an aromatic and vibrant Riesling which has been grown, and not made, to show a beautifully balanced level of sweetness.

Madeleine Stenwreth MW

Few wine industry insiders would disagree that South Africa is the world's most beautiful wine producing country. This is why it is so welcome that over the last decade South Africa's winegrowers have become much more aware of the importance of protecting the wild, biodiverse habitats around their vineyards. The winegrowers' goal should be to get more biodiversity – animals, plants, insects, worms – into the vineyard itself. One simple example is to let geese, chickens or ducks run wild to peck potentially damaging vine grubs away, reducing potential pesticide use.

Another way is to sow a biodiverse mix of flowers and grasses between the vines as so-called "cover crops", to help make vineyards more attractive for both human and beneficial insect visitors. Cover crops also help rain penetrate the soil quicker and deeper, so vines need less irrigation. By providing a green carpet for tractors to drive on, cover crops also help prevent vineyard soils from eroding into dust, a risk in hot climates like South Africa's. Cover crops also help keep soils cooler by blocking the heat of the sun. The cooling effect means grapes can then ripen steadily, without seeing valuable flavours being burnt up. Flowers, herbs, shrubs and trees can also be planted around the vineyard both for beauty and to be used as ingredients for sprays on the vines. Plant teas help vines stay stress-free when bad weather or diseases threaten. And they are cheap, safe and easy to use. Virtually all of Europe's burgeoning number of organic and biodynamic winegrowers routinely use teas made from medicinal plants like stinging nettle, chamomile or willow on their vineyards. Essences made from strong-smelling wild aromatic herbs like garlic, rosemary and thyme are also used to confuse insect pest predators. The extract from just one or two cloves of garlic would be enough to protect several thousand vines.

Ploughing vineyard weeds away using horses and mules instead of tractors is on the increase worldwide, too. The animals are kinder to both soil and vines than expensive gas-guzzling and heavy machinery and long-term animals are cheaper to run and insure. Also, animal manure is the best raw material for compost. Compost is a very cost-effective way of rebuilding damaged vineyard soils. By making their vineyards more biodiverse by using these methods in the right way, South Africa's winemakers can play a leading role in maintaining and enhancing South Africa's natural beauty.

Monty Waldin

BJÖRN RUDNER
PRODUCER : DIRECTOR : CAMERAMAN

INFORMATIONAL
MARKETING
CORPORATE SOCIAL AWARENESS
DOCUMENTARY PRODUCTIONS

Gold Camera and
Silver Screen Awards
U.S. International
Film & Video Festival

083 253 8852 : 021 448 6501

BJRUDNER@CYBERSMART.CO.ZA · WWW.CONTRAST-TV.CO.ZA

Information and statistics on the South African wine industry help provide some context for the current state of play both locally and internationally. Data and information kindly provided by SAWIS.

General Information

- Domestic wine sales increased by 3.1% for the period December 2010-November 2011.

- Also known as the Wine Route, Route 62 leads through the wine-growing areas of Wellington, Tulbagh, Worcester, Robertson and the Klein Karoo and is thus one of the longest wine routes in the world.

- South Africa has the oldest wine industry outside of Europe and the Mediterranean, featuring major white varietals Chardonnay, Chenin Blanc, Riesling, Sauvignon Blanc, Semillon and Viognier. Red varietals include Cabernet Sauvignon and Franc, Cinsault, Merlot, Pinot Noir, Pinotage and Shiraz.

- Today South Africa exports around 400 million litres of wine.

- There are over 112 000 hectares of vineyard in South Africa.

- The 2010 wine grape harvest is estimated at 1 231 400 tons (April 2010).

- South Africa is the 7th largest producer of wine in the world.

- Chenin Blanc is the most widely planted variety in South Africa.

Growth in wineries	2005	2006	2007	2008	2009	2010
Primary wine producers	4360	4183	3999	3839	3667	3596
Wine cellars crushing grapes	581	572	560	585	604	573
Producer cellars	65	65	59	58	57	54
Producing wholesalers	21	17	20	23	23	26

Wines produced (million gross litres)	2006	2007	2008	2009	2010
Wine	709.7	730.4	763.3	805.1	780.7
Rebate	82.1	101.5	86.6	71.4	39.6
Juice	73.2	65.2	72.5	34.7	51.2
Distilling wine	147.9	146.4	166.5	122.1	113.3

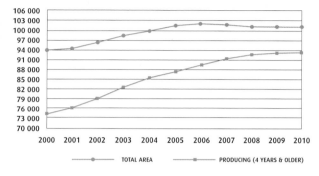

HECTARES | AREA UNDER WINE GRAPE VINEYARDS (Excluding Sultana)

Legend: TOTAL AREA · PRODUCING (4 YEARS & OLDER)

Wine grapes as % of total hectares	2000	2007	2008	2009	2010
Chenin Blanc	24	19	19	18	18
Chardonnay	6	9	8	8	8
Sauvignon Blanc	6	8	9	9	10
Total White	**64**	**56**	**56**	**56**	**56**
Cabernet	9	13	13	12	12
Merlot	5	7	7	7	6
Pinotage	7	6	6	6	6
Shiraz	6	10	10	10	10
Total Red	**36**	**44**	**44**	**44**	**44**

Total SA exports		
Year	Litres	Trend
1996	99 900 000	140
1998	116 800 000	108
2000	138 400 000	108
2001	176 100 000	126
2002	215 800 000	123
2003	237 300 000	110
2004	266 500 000	112
2005	280 084 116	105
2006	271 777 534	97
2007	313 885 785	115
2008	407 319 610	132
2009	389 141 149	96
2010	389 324 000	96

% Total exports by country (litres) (bulk plus bottled)	
2010	**%**
UK	28
Germany	19
Sweden	10
Netherlands	7
Denmark	5
Canada	4
Rest of Africa	4
USA	4
Belgium	3
All Other	16
TOTAL	**100**

REGION	DISTRICT	WARD
GEOGRAPHICAL UNIT: WESTERN CAPE		
BREEDE RIVER VALLEY	BREEDEKLOOF	Goudini Slanghoek
	ROBERTSON	Agterkliphoogte Boesmansrivier Bonnievale Eilandia Hoopsrivier Klaasvoogds Le Chasseur McGregor Vinkrivier
	WORCESTER	Aan-de-Doorns Hex River Valley Nuy Scherpenheuvel
CAPE SOUTH COAST	CAPE AGULHAS	Elim
	ELGIN	No Ward
	OVERBERG	Elandskloof Greyton Klein River Theewater
	PLETTENBERG BAY	No ward
	SWELLENDAM	Buffeljags Malgas Stormsvlei
	WALKER BAY	Bot River Hemel-en-Aarde Ridge Hemel-en-Aarde Valley Sunday's Glen Upper Hemel-en-Aarde Valley
	No district	Herbertsdale Napier Stilbaai East
COASTAL REGION	CAPE POINT	No ward
	DARLING	Groenekloof
	FRANSCHHOEK / FRANSCHHOEK VALLEY	No ward
	PAARL	Simonsberg-Paarl Voor Paardeberg Wellington
	STELLENBOSCH	Banghoek Bottelary Devon Valley Jonkershoek Valley Papegaaiberg Polkadraai Hills Simonsberg-Stellenbosch

REGION	DISTRICT	WARD
	SWARTLAND	Malmesbury Riebeekberg
	TULBAGH	No ward
	TYGERBERG	Durbanville Philadelphia
	No district	Constantia Hout Bay
KLEIN KAROO	CALITZDORP	No ward
	LANGEBERG-GARCIA	No ward
	No district	Montagu Outeniqua Tradouw Tradouw Highlands Upper Langkloof
OLIFANTS RIVER	CITRUSDAL MOUNTAIN	Piekenierskloof
	CITRUSDAL VALLEY	No ward
	LUTZVILLE VALLEY	Koekenaap
	No district	Bamboes Bay Spruitdrift Vredendal
No region	No district	Cederberg Ceres Lamberts Bay Prince Albert Valley Swartberg
GEOGRAPHICAL UNIT: NORTHERN CAPE		
No region	DOUGLAS	No ward
	SUTHERLAND-KAROO	No ward
	No district	Central Orange River Hartswater Rietrivier (Free State)
GEOGRAPHICAL UNIT: EASTERN CAPE		
No region	No district	St Francis Bay
GEOGRAPHICAL UNIT: KWAZULU-NATAL		
No region	No district	No ward

BOBERG (region) For use in respect of fortified wines from Paarl, Franschhoek and Tulbagh.

The appellation system in South Africa is known as the Wine of Origin system. These tables are a useful and handy reference guide to the Geographical Units, Regions, Districts and Wards. Geographical Units are based on provinces and within those there are Regions which are subdivided into Districts and further into Wards.

We thank SAWIS for their permission to reproduce their data above.

Extensive and repeated visits to the world's wine countries make it absolutely clear that South African wine country is arguably the world's most scenic and beautiful. It is exceptionally diverse and is populated with the friendliest of people. South Africa's vineyard families have a warm and welcoming disposition and the traveller is quickly made to feel relaxed and comfortable. This adds to the joy and pleasure of spending time in the exciting wine terroir and exploring endless country delights.

The safest and best option is to choose a bespoke wine tour specialist. Carefully selected, you achieve a non-tourist inside-track experience. **Top 100 SA Wines** specialises in wine country tours with exclusive private visits to **Top 100** awarded vineyards. Walk the vineyards, taste the grapes in season, assess the cellar and maturation approach, taste from barrel and chat to the winemaker or cellarmaster. Then sample a few of their fine wines and if lucky, perhaps an older vintage too. This makes for very special and unique memories.

A helicopter tour is the ultimate option for visiting Cape vineyards if money is not an obstacle. Certainly pricey, it does however afford those lucky participants with a visual feast of unrivalled splendour, colour and texture and is unforgettable. Graphic mountain ranges and valley depictions, a vineyard unravelling into the distance, the scenery is simply spellbinding. It is also a cool way to arrive at the lunch table!

Learning, enjoyment and laughter should be a part of the active day. A special lunch breaks the hard work, enjoyed even more, of course, with a glass or two of paired fine South African wines. All this makes for true relaxation, while the driver or pilot enjoys an espresso! You will arrive back safely, informed, relaxed and armed with heaps of memories and perhaps some fine wine purchases too.

Contact the **Top 100 SA Wine** tour team at **info@top100sawines.com** for more information on flexible and custom wine tour options.

Also quite manageable to do on your own, maps and guides are easy to find and the majority of South Africa's vineyards are open to the public. A suggestion is not to cram too much into the day and take the time for an enjoyable lunch break. Both the experience and the memories are at their best when quality rules quantity.

Please don't drink and drive. Only go self-drive with a nominated driver.

WEEKEND
WINES

liquid pleasure

MERCHANT, TOURS, EVENTS, TASTINGS & IMPORT/EXPORT

CONTACT DETAILS

TEL: +27(0)21 787 9880

robin@weekendwines.co.za

www.weekendwines.co.za

Dependent on where you live, fine wines are typically available from your merchant, specialist wine store, or direct from local vineyards. Certain supermarkets are establishing reputations for having fine wine sections too.

It is fun to browse a quality merchant's shelves and chat to the knowledgeable manager or owner. It can be a great way to learn and to discover new wines and experiences. Look for bin-ends for affordable quality buys, though best check with the store why they are on special.

Vineyard visits are great outings if you live in their proximity. One quickly picks up if the person behind the counter is a for-real wino, or a temporary hired hand with little real knowledge. The experience is typically fun, there is much to learn, and cellar door prices are keen.

Consuming wine

Most wine is bought and then consumed within 48 hours of purchase. At least this is what we are taught. **Top 100 SA Wines** holds different views. Like people, fine wines evolve with age. Rough spots are knocked off, squawkiness and awkwardness disappear. Balance, mettle, personality and finally harmony follow. Mature wines offer so much. Where unsure when to consume a particular wine, seek expert advice. Emailing the producer is one easy way to resolve your questions.

All **Top 100 SA Wines** featured in the 2012/13 consumer guide are outstanding. Enjoyable today, most will last many years. Best open younger wines, particularly Chardonnay and reds, and decant them (a glass water jug will do fine) an hour before consuming.

Typically white wines should be served around 14°C and reds around 19°C. This allows the aromas and flavours to show best. Served colder, many qualities disappear. Served warmer, you then risk alcohols and extraction dominating subtler aspects. No reason on a hot day not to lightly chill and down a simple red. Some rules can be broken!

Don't skimp on glassware. Riedel or Vinum are two fine examples. There are others. Compare for yourself the same wine twice. Use a thick-lipped glass, followed by a fine, thin-lipped large glass. Typically it will appear as if you are appreciating two thoroughly different wines! Make up your own mind once you have conducted this simple, effective test.

Cellaring wine is tremendous fun and will reward hugely. Here are two approaches that can be followed.

1. Cheap 'n cheerful option

Find some space in your house, outbuildings or garage. The key requirement is that it should be dark with stable temperature, free of noise, and cool too. Under the stairs, a cupboard or storeroom will do fine. As long as the criteria above are met you may now claim to own a private cellar!

Top 100 SA wines and other fine wine purchases can now be safely stored to evolve and mature with confidence. Develop a simple spreadsheet to track your stock. A hardcover exercise book is all you need to record your tasting experiences. You are now well on your way to many years of enjoying and sharing with family and friends one of life's truly beautiful experiences: the enjoyment of mature fine wine. You are a winner!

2. Posh option

If you have space, commitment and cash to burn, then building a refrigerated cellar is for you. Bespoke construction will be required. These costs will always be greater than you expect and have not been included in brushstroke figures below. Key to the result will be insulation, special cladding to keep out damp as well as contain internal temperatures. This is expensive. A refrigeration unit is also a key aspect. Typically from Europe, and often custom built to match your cellar size, this will be pricey to buy and install, yet thankfully cheap to run.

Racks, lighting and décor go hand in glove. For a 16m² cellar, a designer stage effect will set you back ZAR 500 000 and upwards, or with simple functionality from ZAR 250 000. Then there is the wine cost. However, your results are guaranteed for life – happy times, a riveting and engaging hobby, even more excuses to celebrate, happy friends and probably a new circle of friends too. Fine wines stored at 12°–14°C will keep in some instances for 50 years or longer. Best not tell your children!

There are other steps inbetween the two above. A compromise is to buy a wine fridge. Effective, quite pricey, sadly not overly attractive, they do, however, do the job.

Kindly note the following information to aid map reading:

- The maps are not all drawn to the same scale.
- North is indicated and does not always face the top of the page.
- Registered South African producers / cellars / wineries have been indicated on the maps with black markers.
- **Top 100 SA Wines 2012/13** winning vineyards are indicated clearly with a yellow marker and black border. ◯

Distances from Cape Town

	km		km		km
Bot River	89	Hermanus	120	Somerset West	45
Caledon	112	Klapmuts	49	Stellenbosch	45
Calitzdorp	380	Kuils River	32	St James	28
Constantia	18	Malmesbury	69	Tulbagh	121
Darling	76	Oudtshoorn	430	Villiersdorp	106
Durbanville	29	Paarl	62	Vredendal	303
Elgin	70	Robertson	159	Wellington	70
Franschhoek	84	Sir Lowry's Pass	54	Worcester	110

Map Key

Top 100 Producer 2012	○	Toll road	═(T)═
Producer / cellar / winery	●	Mountain range	HELDERBERG
Motorway and interchange	━✕━	Airport / airfield	✈
National road and number	N2	Nature reserve	Jonkersberg Nature Reserve
Main road and route number	R27	Place of interest	Cango Caves ●
Secondary road	═══	Dam and river	～◇～

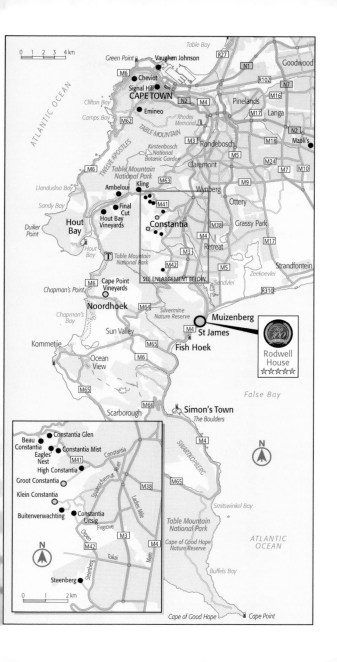

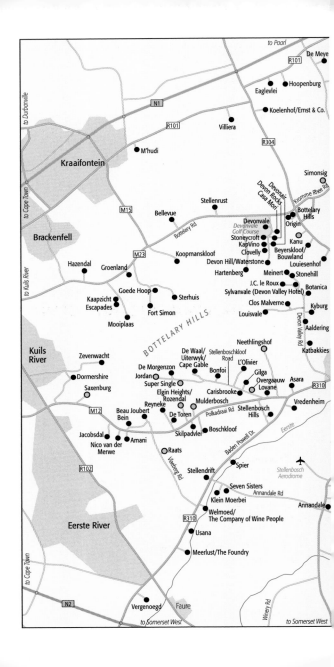

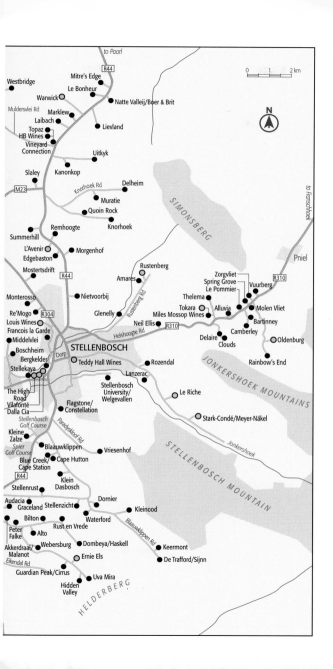

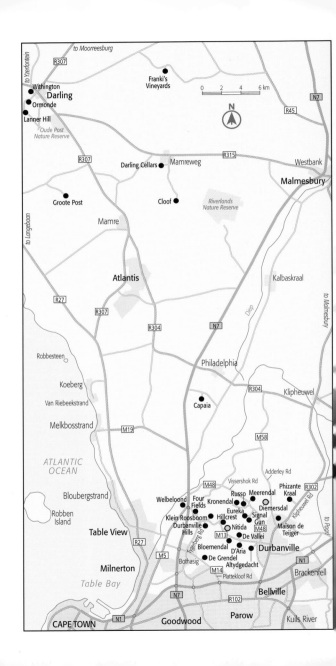

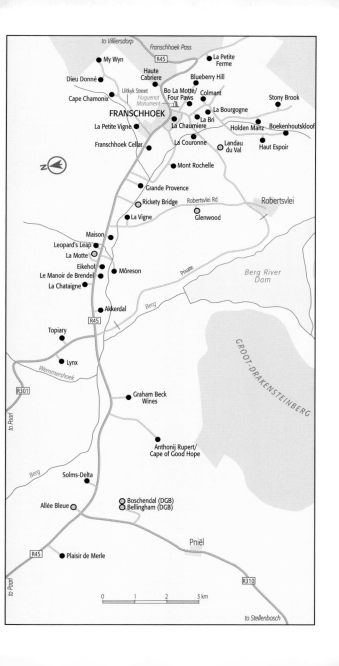

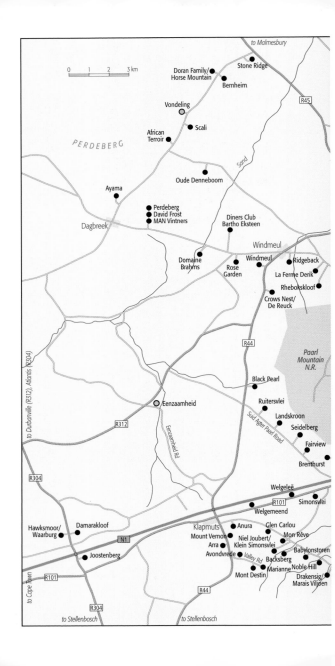

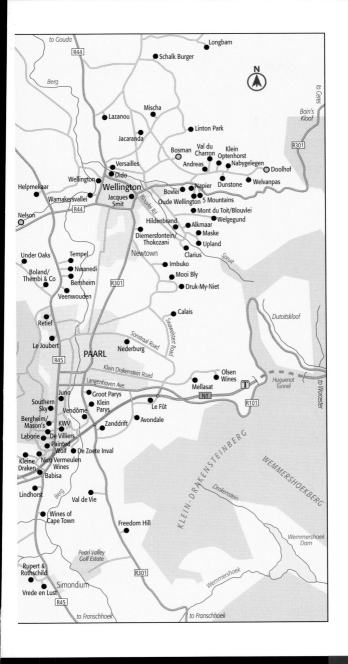

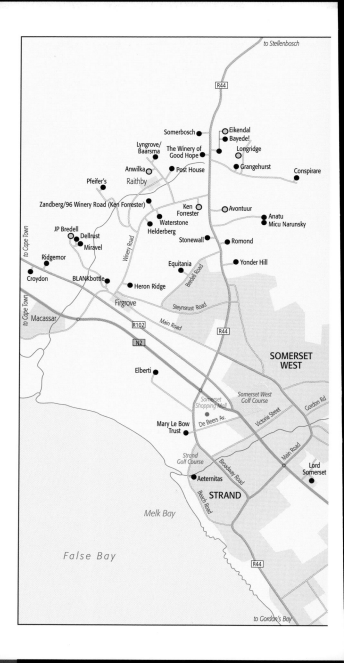

to Stellenbosch

R44

Somerbosch
Eikendal
Bayede!
Lyngrove/
Baarsma
The Winery of
Good Hope
Longridge
Grangehurst
Anwilka
Post House
Conspirare
Pfeifer's
Raithby
Zandberg/96 Winery Road (Ken Forrester)
Ken
Forrester
Avontuur
Anatu
Micu Narunsky
JP Bredell
Dellrust
Waterstone
Helderberg
Miravel
Stonewall
Romond
Ridgemor
Equitania
Yonder Hill
Croydon
BLANKbottle
Beadell Road
Heron Ridge
Winery Road
Firgrove
Steynsrust Road
Macassar
Main Road
R102
R44
N2
SOMERSET
WEST
Elberti
Somerset
Shopping Mall
Somerset West
Golf Course
Gordon Rd
De Beers Av.
Mary Le Bow
Trust
Victoria Street
Main Road
Strand
Golf Course
Broadway Road
Lord
Somerset
Aeternitas
Beach Road
STRAND
Melk Bay
Beach Road
R44
False Bay
to Cape Town
to Cape Town
to Gordon's Bay

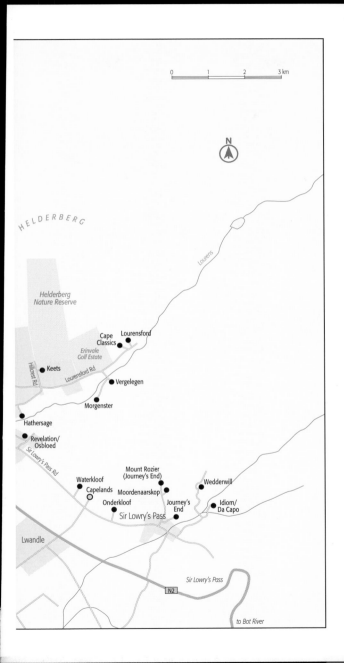

0   1   2   3 km

N

HELDERBERG

Helderberg
Nature Reserve

Lourens

Lourensford

Cape
Classics

Erinvale
Golf Estate

Hillcrest Rd

Keets

Lourensford Rd

Vergelegen

Morgenster

Hathersage

Revelation/
Osbloed

Sir Lowry's Pass Rd

Waterkloof

Capelands

Mount Rozier
(Journey's End)

Moordenaarskop

Onderkloof

Sir Lowry's Pass

Journey's
End

Wedderwill

Idiom/
Da Capo

Lwandle

Sir Lowry's Pass

N2

to Bot River

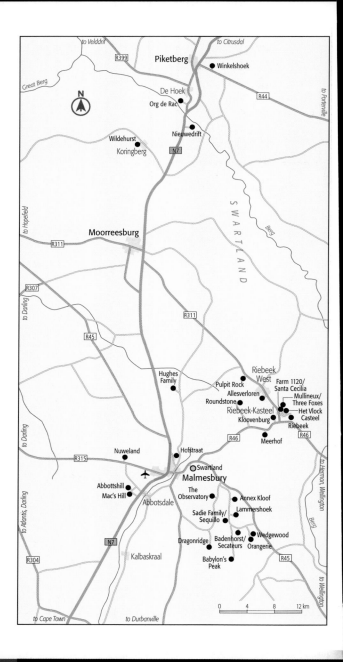

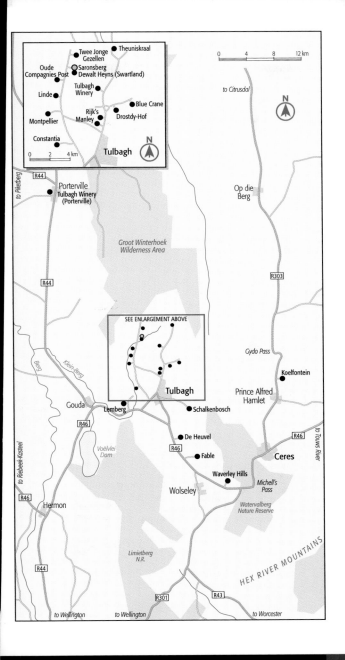

Twee Jonge Gezellen
Theuniskraal
Oude Compagnies Post
Saronsberg
Dewalt Heyns (Swartland)
Linde
Tulbagh Winery
Blue Crane
Rijk's Manley
Drostdy-Hof
Montpellier
Constantia

0 2 4 km
Tulbagh
N

0 4 8 12 km

to Citrusdal
N

R44
Porterville
Tulbagh Winery (Porterville)

Op die Berg

Groot Winterhoek Wilderness Area

R44

R303

SEE ENLARGEMENT ABOVE

Gydo Pass

Koelfontein

Tulbagh

Prince Alfred Hamlet

Berg
Klein-Berg

Gouda
Lemberg
Schalkenbosch

R46
R46
Ceres

Voëlvlei Dam

De Heuvel

R46
Fable

Waverley Hills
Michell's Pass

Wolseley

Hermon

R46

Watervalberg Nature Reserve

R44

Limietberg N.R.

HEX RIVER MOUNTAINS

to Riebeek Kasteel

to Piketberg

R301
R43

to Wellington
to Wellington
to Worcester

to Towns River

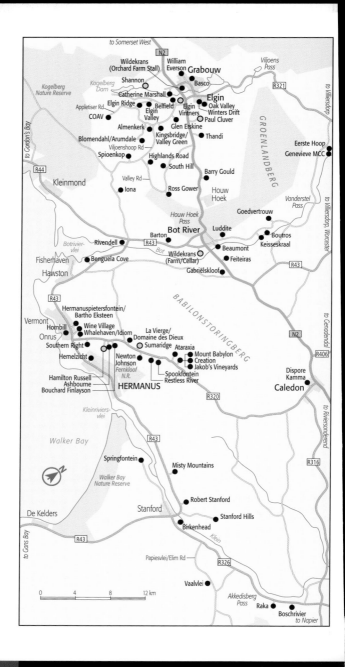

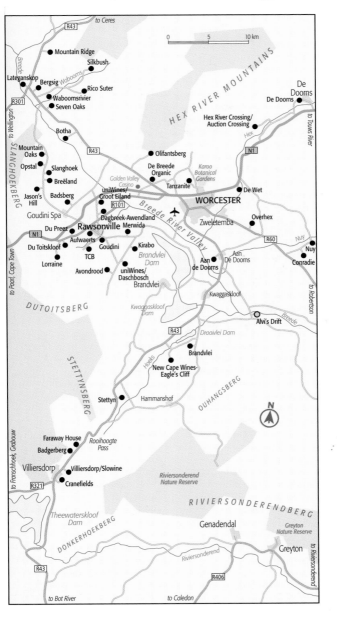

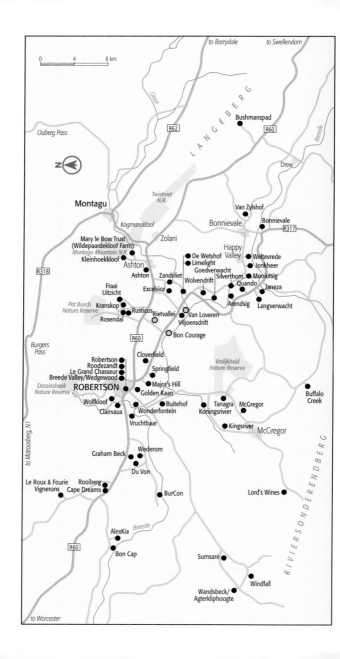

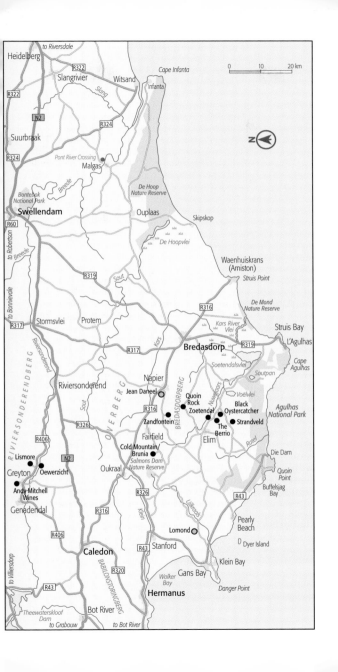

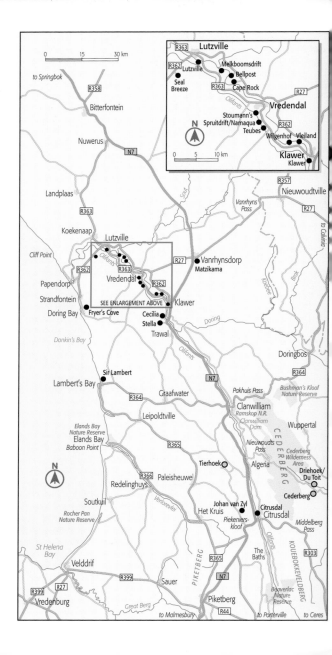

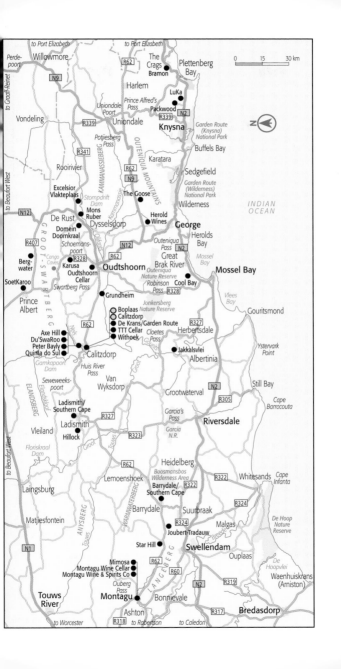

Here we 'de-myth the bunk' around wine jargon and explain some wine terms used generally as well as contained within this book.

Accessible, approachable Flavours and character of the wine are in harmony and it is drinking well now.

Acidity The quality of wine that gives it its crispiness and vitality. A proper balance of acidity must be struck with the other elements of a wine, or else the wine may be said to be too sharp or too flat.

Aftertaste Lingering flavours of a wine after it has been swallowed or removed from the mouth (the longer, the better).

Astringent A puckering, sharp sensation in the mouth attributable to high tannin or excessive acidity.

Austere Usually meaning unyielding, hard to detect qualities. Sometimes, to imply a notable restraint or refinement.

Backbone The wine is well formed and firm.

Baked 'Hot', earthy quality. Usually from very hot temperatures which scorch grapes or from too warm a barrel fermentation or abrasive alcohol levels.

Balance Desirable attribute, indeed key to a fine wine. The wine's acids, alcohol, fruit, tannin, and wood are harmonious.

Barrel fermented Wine fermented in oak barrels as opposed to stainless steel or concrete.

Barrique French term for a 225 litre Bordeaux-style barrel.

Big Weighty full-bodied and expansive character.

Biodynamic Viticulture Biodynamic grape-growing embodies the ideal of ever increasing ecological self-sufficiency and includes ethical-spiritual considerations. This type of viticulture views the farm as a cohesive, interconnected living system.

Blending The mixing of two or more different parcels of wine together by winemakers to produce a consistent finished wine that is ready for bottling.

Body Level of bigness or fullness when on the palate. Often referred to as palate weight.

Bordeaux red blend Wine blended from at least two of Bordeaux varieties: Cabernet Sauvignon, Cabernet Franc, Merlot, Petit Verdot and Malbec.

Bordeaux white blend White wine blend predominantly of Sauvignon Blanc and Semillon but often with a splash of other minor grapes.

Botrytised Offers an extremely concentrated and very sweet flavour with a 'fruit rot' character. From grapes infected with 'noble rot' or botrytis cinerea fungus.

Bottle Age The length of time that wine has been allowed to age and mature in bottle. Also used (positively or negatively) to describe the scent and flavours of a wine.

Brut French term for a very dry champagne or sparkling wine. Drier than extra dry.

Buttery Creamy flavours associated with white wines that have been oaked and most commonly Chardonnays that then offer a dairy rich smoothness.

Canopy Parts of the grape vine above ground, in particular the shoots and leaves.

Cape blend South African red wine blend that includes Pinotage, South Africa's indigenous grape.

Cassis A syrupy liqueur made with blackcurrants, describes wines with a sweet aroma of ripe currants, such as Cabernet Sauvignon and other rich, dark grapes.

Classic Characteristics of the classic wines of Bordeaux, Burgundy or Champagne. Generally this is indicative of the qualities of balance and elegance.

Coarse Abrasive feel, out of balance, excess of undesirable characteristics.

Complexity Denotes multiple layers of aromas, flavours and aftertaste, usually developed further with bottle age.

Concentration Intense flavours or colour.

Confected Constructed, artificial character, unnatural and contrived, even forced.

Corked When a wine is faulty due to oxidation, mould or bacterial infection. Not always caused by the cork. Can offer damp and mouldy character.

Crisp Refers to the palate sense of acidity. In its best sense it implies a clean, fresh or verdant character.

Cultivar Refers to a cultivated grape variety.

Decanting The process of pouring wine from its bottle into a decanter to separate the sediment from the wine and to let the wine breathe.

Deep Depth of intensity, layers and length typically signifying a fine wine.

Demi-sec French term literally meaning 'half dry' but actually implying medium sweetness in sparkling wines.

Dense Tight character often referring to tannin and fruit flavours and texture.

Deposits Evidence that wine has not been fined, filtered or cold-stabilised. Tartrates are harmless and tasteless and generally appear with bottle age.

Dessert wine Varies by region but generally a sweet wine often with a high level of alcohol.

Destemming Process of removing stems from the grapes.

Dried out Lacking in fruit character, tired. A poor vintage or excess age are often the causes.

Dry Wines with zero or very low levels of residual sugar.

Earthy Noticeable character in either aroma or flavour showing fungi, damp leaves, soil, or mouldy roots.

Easy Undemanding, for quaffing.

Elegant Balanced and stylish, refined and classic.

Estate Wine Wine that is produced from grapes grown on the winery's estate with all parts of production completed on the estate.

Extra dry A champagne or sparkling wine with a small amount of residual sugar (slightly sweet). Not as dry as Brut.

Fairtrade Worldwide certification system for agricultural producers that ensures workers are paid a satisfactory wage and that labour terms are fair.

Fermentation The conversion of sugars to alcohol by yeast. In Cape winemaking, cultured yeasts are normally added to secure the process.

Filtration The removal of unwanted particles suspended in wine or grape juice.

Finesse Describes a graceful, polished and subtle wine in fine balance.

Fining Clarification process where flocculants, such as bentonite or egg white, are added to the wine to remove suspended solids. Fining is considered a more gentle method of clarifying a wine than filtering.

Finish Describes the aftertaste of flavour and texture left in your mouth after swallowing.

Firm Signifies tight tannins and an attractive compact frame.

Flabby Loose and unexciting, lacks grip and intensity.

Flat Unexciting, lacks acid and verve, no lift. A bubbly without bubbles.

Fleshy Implies ample, fat, quite showy in aromas, flavours or texture.

Floral, flowery Scent of common flowers such as honeysuckle, jasmine, rose.

Forward Accessible, shows its character immediately.

Fresh Lively, invigorating and youthful, even an imagined effervescence in whites. The wine acid and fruit intensity play the main roles.

Fruity Smells and tastes associated with those of papaya, cantaloupe, grape, mango, pears, berries and others.

Full Typically a big wine, could be high in alcohol, extract and tannins.

Gamey Over-ripe, smelly, referred to as meaty or animal characters.

Grape juice The free-run or pressed juice from grapes.

Gravelly Suggestion of a mineral / earthy quality in some dry white and reds.

Green Usually a puckering and sour or unripe flavour.

Grip Noticeable structure, firm palate. Important in young fine wines with a long life ahead of them, the result primarily of oak and fruit tannins.

Heady Refers to the aromas and implies a lifted intensity.

Hectare A metric measure that equals 10,000 m² (2.471 acres).

Herbaceous Grassy, hay-like, vegetal. Can be an indicator of unripe grapes.

Honey, honeyed Either a subtle character in white wines indicating bottle age, or literally a beeswax or honey flavour typically in off-dry or sweeter whites.

Lean Thin character, can be puckering, lacking the charm and sweetness of fruit.

Lees, leesy Implies a richness and depth of flavour caused by the absorption during 'sur lie', the period the wine is on its lees gathering flavours from the dead yeast cells.

Length Enduring, the wine's flavours endure and echo on the palate well after being swallowed.

Linear Bright acidity and focussed flavors that cut a sharp swath across your palate.

Lively Alive with fresh flavours.

Maceration The contact of grape skins with the must during fermentation.

Malolactic fermentation, MLF Also known as malo, a secondary fermentation in wines by lactic acid bacteria during which tart tasting malic acid is converted to softer tasting lactic acid.

Master of Wine A qualification conferred by The Institute of Masters of Wine, which is based in the UK.

Méthode Cap Classique, MCC Sparkling wine made in the Cape in the same style as French Champagne.

Microclimate The unique climate and geographical conditions of a designated area, such as a vineyard, within a large wine region.

Mousse, bead Bubbles in Champagne or sparkling wine. Pin-prick sized and plentiful long-lasting bead are a good sign.

Mouthfeel, mouthfilling Sensations experienced in the mouth when tasting. Texture and feel in the palate before swallowing.

Must Unfermented grape juice, including pips, skins and stalks.

New World Wines produced outside of the traditional wine growing areas of Europe. In winetasting terms, implies a forward and accessible style, often bold, even extrovert in primary fruit and sometimes wood character.

Nose The aroma or bouquet of a wine.

Oak The most commonly used wood source for fermentation vessel and barrel ageing. Typically French or American.

Oaky Showing noticeable oak aromas or flavours such as char, spice, vanilla or wood smoke.

Old World Wines produced in the traditional wine growing areas of Europe and North Africa. Typical characteristics are balance, complexity, elegance, restraint and subtlety.

Organic winemaking A style of winemaking using organically grown grapes and no chemical fertilisers, herbicides and pesticides.

Palate How the mouth perceives each different, as well as overall combination, of flavours and texture.

Perfume, scent The aromas that the wine offers are stronger than expected.

Phenolic compounds Compounds found in the seeds, skins and stalks of grapes that contribute vital characteristics to the colour, texture and flavour of wine. Tannins are the most notable phenolic compounds.

Pre-fermentation maceration The time prior to fermentation that the grape must spend in contact with its skins. This technique may enhance some of the varietal characteristics of the wine and leech important phenolic compounds out from the skin. This process can be done either cold (also known as a "cold soak") or at warmer temperatures.

Pump over Circulating the fermenting juice from the bottom of the tank over the skin cap that forms during fermentation to ensure optimal extraction and prevent bacterial spoilage.

Punch down Breaking and pushing the skin cap back into the fermenting wine to increase extraction of colour and flavour.

Pyrazines A group of aromatic compounds in grapes that contribute to some of the green herbaceous notes in wine.

Racking The process of drawing wine off the sediment, such as lees, after fermentation and moving it into another vessel.

Reductive Without exposure to oxygen. Wine in an unevolved, unoxidised state is said to be "reductive"; usually with a tight, sometimes unyielding character.

Rhône-style blend Red wine blend generally led with Syrah (Shiraz) and usually with Grenache and Mourvedre or other grapes predominant in the Rhône region of France.

Rich Flavourful and generous character, often big natured and intense.

Robust One step up from rich, a full-bodied and muscular nature.

Round Well balanced, indeed comfortable within itself.

Screw cap An alternative to cork for sealing wine bottles, comprising a metal cap that screws onto threads on the neck of a bottle.

Sec French for dry, except in the case of Champagne, where it means semi-sweet.

Secondary fermentation Most commonly the term is used to refer to the continuation of fermentation in a second vessel, for instance moving the wine from a stainless steel tank to an oak barrel.

Sharp, tart Unbalanced acid or the consequence of using unripe grapes.

Simple One-dimensional, little flavour or character. Why bother.

Single vineyard wine A single vineyard designated wine is a wine produced from officially registered vineyards, no larger than 6 hectares in size and planted with a single variety.

Sommelier A wine expert who generally works in fine restaurants. They will be knowledgeable about wines, food pairings and often other beverages such as spirits, beers and cocktails.

Stabilisation The process of decreasing the volatility of a wine by removing particles that may cause unwanted chemical changes after the wine has been bottled. This is often achieved by fining, filtration, or adding sulphur dioxide.

Stalky Denotes a bitter and unripe flavour, often the result of crushing the grapes with their stems.

Stewed Cooked or over-ripe aromas or flavours, even a porty character, unpleasant and heavy in an unfortified wine.

Structure Implies a noteworthy presence and includes the wine's acid, alcohol, fruit and tannin make up.

Stylish Balanced and harmonious composition that exudes pedigree.

Supple Flavoursome wine offering enjoyable characters, flexible enough to suit many moments.

Sur lie French term for 'on the lees' that involves prolonged ageing on the dead yeast cells.

Sustainable viticulture Farming method that limits the environmental impact of making wines. Based on the idea that farming should be economically viable, socially supportive and ecologically sound.

Tannic Prominent, mostly wood tannins, promote a grippy, pithy hard character or structure on the palate.

Tannin Phenolic compound that gives wine a bitter, dry, or puckery feeling in the mouth.

Tasting flight Refers to a selection of wines presented for the purpose of sampling and comparison.

Tension Denotes a nervous or edgy sense, where acid and fruit interplay tingle the tongue.

Terpenes, terpenoid Powerful turpentine-like aromas found in Gewürztraminer and Riesling, which can exacerbate into an oily character with time.

Terroir French for 'soil', the physical and geographical characteristics of a particular vineyard site that give the resultant wine its unique properties.

Texture Implies the feel of the wine in the mouth e.g. acidic, velvety, hot. A tactile character.

Toasty Common description of pleasant charry character, the result of barrel maturation.

Varietal Wines made from a single grape variety.

Viniculture The art and science of making wine. Also called oenology. Not to be confused with viticulture.

Vinification The process of making grape juice into wine.

Vintage A vintage wine is one made from grapes that were all, or primarily, grown and harvested in a single specified year.

Viticulture The cultivation of grapes. Not to be confused with viniculture.

Yeast A micro-organism present on the skins of grapes that reacts with the sugars inside and results in the production of ethyl alcohol during fermentation.

Yeasty Fresh baked bread aromas consistent with wooded whites and Champagne.

Yield In any farming capacity, the quantity of quality fruit that a parcel of land renders after a harvest. In terms of winemaking it is the quantity of grapes that a vineyard can produce per hectare of land to produce the level of quality desired.